INSIDE
10 RILLINGTON
PLACE

INSIDE
10 RILLINGTON PLACE

PETER THORLEY

MIRROR BOOKS

First published by Mirror Books in 2020

Mirror Books is part of Reach plc
10 Lower Thames Street
London EC3R 6EN

www.mirrorbooks.co.uk

Print ISBN 978-1-913406-11-0
eBook ISBN 978-1-913406-12-7

Typeset by Danny Lyle

Printed and bound in Great Britain by
CPI Group (UK) Ltd, Croydon, CR0 4YY

A CIP catalogue record for this book is available from the British Library.

1 3 5 7 9 10 8 6 4 2

Cover images: Alamy

Dedicated to the memory of my
beloved sister and niece

Contents

The following events are based on my own experiences, research, official documents and firm beliefs about what really happened in 10 Rillington Place. This is my truth.

Foreword
By Lea Thorley

Peter and I have been together for more than half a century. We met in 1963 and married two years later. Ever since those early days, and despite the many ups and downs that life throws at you, we have truly been soulmates and are still very much together.

Peter can now tell the real story of 10 Rillington Place, providing ultimate closure to a lifetime of sadness. The deaths of his sister Beryl and niece Geraldine haunted him, and the subsequent inquests and trials have done little to numb the pain.

Now, Peter will finally be able to set the record straight once and for all and reveal what he has believed for 70 years to be the truth.

Peter's peace of mind, despite it being so late in time, is of paramount importance. It has been worth every minute of the 35 years it has taken us to explore the entire history of this horrific and notorious murder case that took place at 10 Rillington Place back in November 1949.

For decades, Peter has seen third-hand accounts of the case reproduced in the media, containing the same mistakes and prejudices about the course of events and the victims. He has truly suffered and struggled to come to terms with the tragedy every day, since learning that his beloved sister and niece had been found brutally strangled and dumped in a grimy wash house.

The reality of 10 Rillington Place was far removed from what you may have been led to believe in the past. We have gone through hundreds of authentic documents, original records, papers and photographs of all kinds and we have worked closely together over many years to establish the final truth. We have both been overcome with emotion, shedding tears at the monotonous repeats of misleading films and documentaries about the case on television.

Reading this book, I believe that you will be able to understand completely the torment Peter has gone through, and why it became necessary to devote so much time to researching the tragic lives of Beryl and Geraldine. Keeping them in our thoughts is so important.

At the time of writing Peter is 85 years old and harbours his anguish with dignity. The theories surrounding Beryl and Geraldine's death remain contentious, and doubts still linger across the nation as to whether Reg Christie or Timothy Evans killed Peter's sister and niece. Millions of words have been written about the case but, in his heart, Peter has always known the truth.

Foreword

For me, hearing his accounts of being in and out of Rillington Place has always held a certain fascination and intrigue. He clearly remembers the inside of the house where Beryl, Geraldine, Timothy Evans and Reg Christie all lived, and he is one of the last first-hand witnesses of what life was like under that roof.

Finally, this book brings us closer than ever before to the truth of what really happened inside 10 Rillington Place.

Chapter 1
Hatred in the House

It was a cold October night in 1949. Timothy Evans, my brother-in-law, finished his last drink after a usual lengthy session in the Kensington Park Hotel. It was closing time, and a night of bragging and heavy drinking had come to an end.

He set off on the two-minute walk along St Mark's Road to Evans's home, 10 Rillington Place in Notting Hill. There waiting for Evans was my 19-year-old sister Beryl, who had the misfortune to be his young wife, and their baby daughter, Geraldine.

The streets were run down and recovering from the wartime bombing of London. Partly demolished houses lined his route as he approached the cul-de-sac. Evans stumbled, ungainly on his feet.

Most gas lights in the houses had been extinguished with the time approaching 11pm. At 10 Rillington Place, everyone had gone to bed. The Christies' lights on the ground floor were off.

1

Mr Kitchener's flat on the first floor was in darkness, as he had gone to hospital for an eye operation earlier in the month. Mr Kitchener was not a well man.

All was quiet on the second floor, where Beryl waited, knowing another dreadful night lay in store.

I was told all about those violent nights. Beryl described them to me in great detail, though I was only 14 and couldn't always take it all in. But I loved my big sister Beryl so much, and I knew how afraid she was of Evans.

The key turned in the lock, below a rusty black knocker. The door was a faded shade of dark green. Evans was quickly inside and hobbled up the narrow staircase to the top flat, with his distinctive limp from a childhood foot problem.

Voices were raised almost at once. Evans yelled. Beryl shouted back. Evans yelled even louder, blaming my sister for their financial troubles.

Then whack. He struck her hard with his fists. Again. And again.

Gradually the noise abated, and a typical evening in 10 Rillington Place came to a close.

Timothy Evans regularly beat my sister, and blamed her for not running a proper household. Evans was working as a food delivery driver, earning about seven pounds a week with overtime. That wasn't bad money back then. The rent was 10 shillings a week – 50p in today's money. They were also paying hire purchase costs for the furniture, adding up to just over seven shillings a week. Beryl had had to give up her job to look after the baby, so the family were under severe financial pressure during the dismal post-war years.

But rather than saving his earnings, Evans spent most of them on drinking and gambling.

The neighbours were repeated witnesses to his violent behaviour. The loud late-night rows were continuous. One lady, Mrs Rosina Swan, who lived next door at No. 9, recalled seeing the two of them fighting; Beryl was struggling to get away from her husband. Another neighbour who lived directly opposite said she witnessed a commotion on several occasions. From what she could see, during one particular incident, Evans was trying to push his wife out of the window.

One of Beryl's friends, Lucy Endicott, told many people about the continual disturbances inside 10 Rillington Place. Lucy was said to have been 'lodging' with Evans and Beryl – though heaven only knows how they arranged themselves in that tiny flat. It was Lucy who had set Beryl up with Evans in the first place; but now, with Lucy staying in the flat, Beryl's suspicions were growing that something was going on between her and Timothy Evans.

On one raucous evening, Evans was screaming and shouting as usual. Lucy was present at the flat, as well as Timothy Evans's mother Thomasina Probert, and soon they were in the thick of it too. Evans was threatening Beryl in the ugliest terms.

'I'll do you in!' he bellowed.

Beryl was petrified. In a panic, she hurried out of the flat and down the stairs to see Ethel Christie, who lived with her husband Reg on the ground floor, and asked her what she should do. Ethel told her to call the police, and asked her husband to accompany Beryl to the local phone box.

Beryl knew that Lucy and Evans had been to the cinema the night before, came back to the flat and both slept in the kitchen, no doubt on the floor. Beryl believed they had sex that night, and when she returned from the phone box, she confronted Lucy, accusing her of carrying on with her husband. Lucy slapped her in the face. Beryl could deliver a vicious slap herself, but on this occasion decided not to make things any worse.

A constable arrived at Rillington Place as the fracas continued between Evans and Beryl. The officer ordered all concerned to 'cool it'. Mrs Probert left for home, while Beryl was advised by the constable to attend a magistrates' court, where she received advice from a probation officer.

Meanwhile Evans departed with Lucy, leaving Beryl and Geraldine alone in the flat. Evans stayed with Lucy, continuing their affair until a few days later when she decided to end it. Lucy had also found herself on the receiving end of Evans's violent behaviour, and she returned to her mother's house.

Evans continued with his heavy drinking, late nights and constant lies. He often went out to the pub with my 17-year-old brother Basil, who was the spitting image of me, three years older and six inches shorter.

My beloved sister's life had become intolerable. I could sense hatred in the house every time I went to visit her and my sweet niece.

A regular visitor of Beryl's was her old school friend Joan Vincent. Joan was close to Beryl, and had become deeply concerned for her wellbeing. Joan's husband Charles was equally worried for Beryl after a conversation with Timothy Evans in the wake of his affair with Lucy. Evans told him: 'I'm going off the track. If I ever get hold of that Lucy Endicott, I'll smash her up or run her down with my van.'

Charles knew that Beryl had had to defend herself against Evans on several occasions. He heard Evans threatening Beryl – 'I'll do you in!' – but he was sure Evans would never actually go that far.

Beryl desperately wanted to get away from him. She needed to leave their hellish home. But she didn't have the money to escape on her own.

* * *

The previous year, a few months after Beryl and Timothy Evans moved into 10 Rillington Place in March 1948, I made regular visits to see her and enjoy hugs with my smiley niece.

I chose my words carefully.

'How are you getting on in the new place?' I asked Beryl. 'People have been saying Tim is causing trouble.'

'The flat's fine. Yes, I'm still having some problems with Tim and his drinking. Neighbours seem nice enough. I don't really see much of Mr Kitchener on the first floor. He's always in hospital and I've only seen him a couple of times.'

Mr Kitchener had been a tenant on the first floor since 1918. He had been born in 1877 and married Sarah Ann Kitchener. She wasn't around when I visited, so I presumed she was dead or they had separated. Mr Kitchener had serious eyesight problems, and he could only see people as dim objects. When I went round to visit Beryl, he was usually in hospital having treatment.

'The Christies seem to be pleasant enough,' Beryl told me. 'If I nip out to the shops, Mrs Christie looks after Geraldine.'

Reg and Ethel Christie from the ground-floor flat looked after my niece quite often to give Beryl a break. When Evans and Beryl went to the pictures, Christie and Ethel always agreed to keep an eye on the baby. If Geraldine was asleep, Ethel would go upstairs and check on her regularly, and when Geraldine woke up, she would bring the baby downstairs and keep her amused until her mum and dad returned.

Reg and Ethel seemed to enjoy looking after Geraldine, as they had no children of their own. They did have a friendly little mongrel called Judy, though. When Geraldine was being looked after by the Christies, Judy would run in and out of the house, making Geraldine giggle out loud.

Whenever I came to visit Beryl, Reg Christie would open the door to me. If Beryl was out, he invited me into his flat for tea and sticky buns while we waited for her. He seemed fond of children like me, and always let me play ball with Judy out in the garden.

Christie seemed genuinely fond of Beryl too. In fact, he was quite protective of her, because he knew only too well how bad-tempered and violent Evans could be.

'He's very kind to me,' Beryl told me. 'I feel safe when he's around.'

Beryl feared her husband a great deal, but she had no fear of Christie. She said there was nothing improper in Christie's manner towards her, and she regarded him as a 'perfect gentleman'. From what I saw, he always treated her kindly.

The Christies were quiet people who kept themselves to themselves and didn't have many visitors. They used to go to the cinema a short distance away, and were seen regularly in the library. Ethel would occasionally visit her sister, who lived in Sheffield.

Back then, Reg Christie was regarded by many in the area as a man of 'certain principle'. He was clean-shaven, and very particular with his personal hygiene despite the limited facilities of the time. He was never seen scruffily dressed, usually attired in a suit, collar and tie and highly polished shoes. I was told by neighbours that, when a collection took place for a family who had lost a child, he was particularly generous and sympathetic.

I bumped into Reg Christie several times a week in 10 Rillington Place. I enjoyed passing the time there. Often when I arrived, Reg and Ethel were both sitting down in the kitchen, so I would sit down in a peculiar-looking rope chair next to them for a chat. It was an old deck chair with strands of rope installed to take your weight. Christie had replaced the canvas with clever rope work. He was a bit of a handyman, always taking up little projects around the house.

If Beryl was out for a walk with Geraldine, Ethel would make tea for us all while we waited for them to come back. Sometimes Ethel herself was away visiting her sister in Sheffield, so I would be alone with Reg Christie, and he would make us a brew. He usually produced a plate of sticky buns alongside the tea, much to my delight. Ethel kept jams, sauces and all sorts of other ingredients neatly stored in the cupboards under the dresser.

Ethel and Reg always used a teapot with loose tea, as teabags weren't in fashion, and they had matching cups and saucers and tea plates. I was never given a bun in my fingers – it always came on a plate. The kettle of water was boiled on the gas stove, as there was no electricity in the house.

Over our snacks, Christie told me what he'd been doing during the day. He might have been to the library, or on a trip to see the doctor for one of his many ailments. Sometimes he had been to the cinema with Ethel the previous evening, so he told me all about the film they had seen. They didn't seem to go out for meals, drinks or anything; they just went to the nearby Royalty cinema and back home again. I described my lessons at school and my homework. I told him that English was my best subject, although I liked History and Geography too.

We sat at the table to play snap and rummy, the old card games. It kept us occupied while as I waited for Beryl to get back. We were pretty well matched at rummy, and honours were generally even. We never played for money – we were just playing to amuse ourselves.

Christie had a soft, whispery voice, and always spoke quietly. I remember our games of snap very clearly. If Christie put down the Queen of Spades and I added the Queen of Hearts, he would rasp, 'Snap.' It was quite a contrast to my yelps when I won. Ethel would look round and smile as she put the plates back in the dresser or started to prepare the supper. I tried to play one or two tricks on Christie, trying to make him guess which card I was holding, but he usually saw through my mischief.

While we were playing cards, he used to say: 'You have to watch that Evans. He's a nasty character, always shouting at Beryl. Keep an eye on him.'

I took Reg Christie at his word. I already knew from Beryl how dreadfully Evans treated her.

Beryl wasn't able to go out very often; for a start, there wasn't the money. On the odd occasion, she went to the pictures with Timothy or her friends. When Beryl arrived home one night after a rare evening out, Timothy, by now totally out of control after his usual extended drinking session, seemed to think that baby Geraldine had been left at Rillington Place all alone. Her drunken husband snarled: 'I'll give you a bloody good hiding, my girl, for going to the pictures and leaving the baby.'

Beryl protested that she had left Geraldine with Ethel Christie to look after her, but Evans wouldn't listen. He set about her and began striking her across the face and body. His attacks were incredibly brutal, and Beryl, as so often, was left marked and bruised from his beatings.

As his temper grew and grew, Evans made that same chilling threat he often used: 'I'll put you through the bloody window.'

*   *   *

Evans's affair with Lucy was over, but his and Beryl's problems were spiralling out of control. The couple were getting into more and more debt during that October of 1949. That month, Reg Christie opened the front door downstairs to a man who said he had come to collect arrears for the furniture that the couple had on hire purchase. As Evans was out at work, Christie paid what was outstanding. When Evans returned home, Christie caught him in the doorway.

'I had a caller earlier who wanted money. I don't want people demanding money at the door. I've got my reputation to think of. I'm expecting you to reimburse me.'

'It's all Beryl's fault,' Evans muttered. 'I'm going upstairs to sort her out.'

In reality, it was Evans who had drunk and gambled the money away, leaving my poor sister with a mere pittance to look after the family.

Another tremendous row followed. The fights had become a normal occurrence, and it seemed as if Evans was using the domestic unrest as a devious tactic, an excuse to go out drinking again – with more violence assured when he returned home drunk night after night.

When I went round to visit Beryl, play with Geraldine, have tea with Christie and run around with Judy the dog, I would see Beryl's bruises and ask her what had happened. She told me everything about her husband's dangerous habits and his vicious violent streak, but what could I do? I was still a child, only just a teenager, still living at home with my family.

I was old enough, however, to take in the seriousness of the situation. I knew about the rows and the blows being inflicted on Beryl. Whilst I felt powerless to do anything myself, I told my father that I was concerned for Beryl's welfare. It had got so bad that, during one loud and violent row, neighbours started knocking on the walls. Even Christie intervened at one stage, marching upstairs and reading the riot act.

'If this continues, you will have to leave,' he told them.

I had reason to be worried, and I hoped my father or brother would intervene before anything disastrous happened.

But Dad had other plans.

Our family had moved out of London to Brighton a few months earlier, although I still managed regular trips on the train to see Beryl and Geraldine. I had to keep making sure they were all right, for my own peace of mind as well as Beryl's safety.

One day that October, at home in Brighton, Dad took me aside for a word.

'Son, I've got some news. I'm sending you to New Zealand.'

I was stunned. 'New Zealand? That's on the other side of the world, isn't it?'

'It's for the best,' he insisted. 'It's a child emigration scheme. You'll enjoy it. All that fresh air, away from the smoke and fog here. You'll come back as a man.'

I couldn't believe it. Why was he sending me away, especially when our family needed each other most? I had tried to make it clear to him that Beryl was in danger, and that we needed to be there for her.

But he didn't explain his reasons. He simply told me that it cost £10, and at that moment I knew I had no say in the matter.

I wondered whether the new lady in his life wanted me out of the way.

What could I do? Everything was signed and sealed. All I knew was that I would be leaving before the end of the year, within a month or two, at the worst possible time.

I felt shocked, betrayed, afraid of the unknown, unwanted and unloved. I was still only a child, really. And I was frightened about what was going on in the Evans household. The atmosphere inside 10 Rillington Place was becoming more and more toxic.

Evil, pure evil, lurked inside.

Christie and Ethel in the garden at 10 Rillington Place.

Chapter 2

Tea and Buns with Uncle Reg

What Evans didn't know was that he wasn't the only inhabitant of 10 Rillington Place with something to hide.

I have learned a great deal about John Reginald Halliday Christie over the years. I thought I'd got to know him quite well. I knew him simply as 'Uncle Reg', a kindly gentleman who plied me with tea and sticky buns. That was what he was like. He struck me as a man who was kind to children.

John Christie's father was a carpet designer called Ernest John Christie. By all accounts, Ernest was a hard taskmaster, punishing the children for trivial offences in the house. He would give them 'a good hiding' – although we shouldn't read too much into that. Discipline in those days was tough, and children did often get fierce slaps with the hand or sometimes a slipper on the bare backside.

When John Christie came into the world, the family was already flourishing. He had five older siblings: Percy was 16, Florence 14,

Effie 12, Elsie eight and Winifred two. Phyllis arrived shortly after Reg to complete the set. In those days, people seemed to be called by all sorts of different names: Florence was known as Cissy and Phyllis was called Dolly. As John grew older, people started to call him Reggie, or Reginald on more formal occasions. Over the years, his Christian name was slimmed down to 'Reg'.

The Halliday part of his name came from his mother, who was christened Mary Hannah Halliday. All their children had 'Halliday' as part of their names. Mary was the daughter of David Halliday, a local Liberal councillor who was also the owner of a boot-making factory.

The family lived at Black Boy House in the Claremount area of Halifax, West Yorkshire. The building was in Turner Lane, an unmade road at the time. The house used to be a pub called the Black Boy – not an uncommon name for hostelries then. There are a few still around England, although some have dropped the name for obvious reasons.

At the age of eight, Christie's grandfather died, and young Reg saw him lying in his open casket. Christie was intrigued, looking at the body of the old man. After that he was seen wandering around graveyards, smelling the flowers left by relatives.

Reg Christie left school at 15 with a certificate, reflecting his abilities, and found work as a projectionist at Green's Picture Hall. He also worked occasionally in the warehouse of the boot-making firm.

He never told me, of course, but Christie was haunted by an early sexual failure as a teenager. At the age of 16, Christie was matched up by his friends with a young lady of some experience in a lover's lane. It was at Savile Park in Halifax, a place that had acquired the nickname of 'The Monkey Run'. His mates had no problem in performing, but Christie felt under too much pressure and his manhood failed to rise to the occasion.

The girl and her friends had a field day mocking him. Christie soon became known as 'Reggie no-dick', 'Reggie no-cock' and 'can't-get-it-up-Christie'. Those taunts must have hurt and stayed with him for the rest of his life.

There is some suggestion that this psychological torment led to an inability for Christie to have a normal sexual relationship. That early experience made him dread sex with women, I believe, and he had to be in complete control in order to perform. This intimate, highly personal detail of his life would turn out to be very significant later, in uncovering the man beneath the surface of what I saw on my visits to 10 Rillington Place.

Rillington Place wasn't far from the North Kensington Central School, where I was a hard-working pupil at the time when Beryl and Timothy Evans moved in during 1948. I'd won a scholarship there from Solomon Wolfson Jewish School. The two schools I had attended were just round the corner from each other: leaving Solomon Wolfson, I would pass the Royalty cinema next door, walk across Ladbroke Grove, continue straight, and the Central School was there on my left.

I would appear at Christie's front door after school in my blazer and long trousers – I'd passed the shorts stage by then – to see Beryl and Geraldine.

It was all gas lights in 10 Rillington Place, with no electricity at all. The Christies had a kitchen, bedroom and a lounge, and everyone in the building used the wash house and toilet area to the rear.

The layout of Christie's flat, and what was inside, is still imprinted on my mind. The rooms were small, and I can remember them as if it all happened yesterday. Coming in through the front door, I had the choice of going up the stairs, turning into their front room, or walking along the passage past their bedroom. The front room had a settee, an armchair and a fireplace. There wasn't an awful lot in there.

The chairs placed at the table in the kitchen had the old straight backs. He used to have his meals at that table, and so would Ethel. There was no proper dining table; the place wasn't big enough for that. There was a dresser with plates and other crockery on it, and a kitchen range.

Uncle Reg fancied himself as a photographer. He had a proper camera, a German make, and it was his pride and joy. If there were local festivities, he would be the first to appear with his lens, ready to capture the action. He even loaned his camera to a local group for their annual outing. He showed me pictures he'd taken of Ethel in their younger days. They weren't bad, though some were a bit out of focus. Others had dark shadows and didn't look too sharp.

Heading out through the back door, there was the wash house and toilet in a little yard. Then there was an old broken wooden gate that was never closed, leading out into the small garden. At the bottom of the garden there was a high wall shielding a garage area.

There was no fence, maybe a trellis against the wall. It was a rough patch of ground with lumps of soil and rock, surrounded by the brick wall. I played out there with Christie's dog Judy many times, throwing balls for her in the garden.

If anyone knocked at the front door, Christie would usually get up and walk straight down the passage from the kitchen. As I remember, there never was a 'spyhole' in the kitchen door, or any other door or wall, come to that. I've read several accounts of there being some sort of 'peephole'. That wasn't the case. However, the kitchen door was half glazed with two parallel lengths of glass, and it was covered by a curtain. If we were in the kitchen and he got up to answer the door, I would have a look through the curtain to see who it was, like any other nosey kid.

To see Beryl I would go through the front door and up the narrow stairs to the left. I would pass Mr Kitchener's place on the first floor, then reach Beryl's flat on the second floor.

There were just two rooms on the second floor. On the left was the kitchen, with a window overlooking the garden. Across the landing was a door into their front room – it was also their bedroom. Opening the door, the baby's cot was right in front of me. I was Uncle Peter to Geraldine, of course.

The window in the bedroom overlooked Rillington Place, and I often saw children playing in the street below. When you see actual pictures of Rillington Place, there are usually children playing outside.

The buildings in Rillington Place weren't new. They dated back to 1869, with a number of builders involved in the project. Numbers 1 to 10 ran along on one side, and 11 to 20 on the other. No. 10 was close to a large chimney, protruding out of Bartle's iron foundry.

Uncle Reg was knowledgeable about the area's history and how Rillington Place came about, and he told me all about it over tea. Not unlike today, developers were speculating and looking for the most profitable areas to build houses, and the manor of Notting Barns was an attractive area for building work in the mid-19th century. Colonel Matthew Chitty Downes St Quintin was the freeholder; he had spread his wings from Malton in Yorkshire – coincidentally, the same county where Christie grew up.

Not far from Malton lies the village of Rillington, which is evidently where the name came from. Long leases were granted to the developers who paid annual ground rent for land in the

Notting Barns area. The St Quintin Estate in North Kensington traces its roots all the way back to the colonel; he had serious mental issues, and his relatives took over the affairs of his estates in the late 1850s.

Uncle Reg told me that building work all around Rillington Place was affected by a financial meltdown. The so-called 'banker's banker', Overend, Gurney and Company, collapsed in 1866. They owed £11 million, worth well over £1 billion in today's values. The company continued to make investments, without building up reserves of cash. They found themselves in deep trouble when stocks and bonds collapsed.

The bank had invested heavily in private railway companies, which took a big hit. Rillington Place was intended for fairly well-off families from those railway firms, who were now struggling in the financial collapse. It meant that more working-class tenants lived in Rillington Place, several to a room. The rental value for the properties was £28, although they weren't all occupied until 1871. That pattern continued as the area became more and more run down, particularly during the Second World War.

Reg said the census of 1871 revealed that a family with the name of 'Coplin' lived at 15 Rillington Place. That name was written down in error, because the name was actually 'Chaplin'. Charles, Charlie Chaplin's father, lived there when he was eight years old.

Christie told me all about the star of silent films. 'Charlie Chaplin was born in London, but I'm not sure where,' he said. 'He became world famous and even wrote and directed his own films. I saw *The Great Dictator* at the Royalty the other night. It's an attack on people like Hitler and Mussolini. You'll have to see it.'

I didn't know much about Charlie Chaplin, except that he dressed as a tramp and made those iconic films in Hollywood. If I wanted to know more, I knew who to ask.

Around the same time, the family of James Bartle, who owned the nearby Western Iron Works, had lived at 3 Rillington Place. Christie told me about the Bartles to show me that, initially, the houses were occupied by well-to-do people and not divided into flats.

Criminologist F. Tennyson Jesse gives a rather harsh description of the street during the time of the Christies' occupation: '10 Rillington Place was a tiny shabby house, where the paint needed renewing, where there was no bathroom and only one WC on the garden level for all the inhabitants. Being a cul-de-sac, Rillington Place was the natural playground of the children of the neighbourhood. On summer days when the evenings are mild, the housewives sit out on broken chairs or on the kerb edge and call to acquaintances passing in slippers and curlers. The yellow brick of the mean terraced houses, which face each other across the littered street, is stained and the doors and windows are ill fitting, for the foundations are gradually sinking. At the end of the cul-de-sac is a wall and behind it shows an ugly factory chimney.'

Another description, published during the period, states: 'No. 10 is the last house on the left-hand side. There are no cellars, the staircase is narrow and it is impossible for anybody to do much about the house without the other inhabitants hearing. On the ground floor there is an ugly bay Victorian window to the front room of the house, surrounded by crumbling sandstone.'

Of course, so soon after the end of the Second World War, it didn't seem anything like as bad as that to me.

When Ethel went shopping she would just use the corner shop, normally. There were no supermarkets like we have now. If she went further afield she would shop at a greengrocer, baker, general store or a newsagent. As with most people, she would get provisions in every day, because there were no fridges or freezers back then. Most houses had a wooden box with a wire net door, usually fixed to a wall outside in the back yard and preferably out of the sun, which helped to keep meat, butter, eggs and milk cool.

Ethel and Beryl would return from the shops with freshly baked crusty loaves bought from the local bakery at a price of four old pennies and a halfpenny each. They were still warm as they sat on the baker's counter. The bread in houses at the time was usually kept in enamel bread bins and sliced as needed. When I used to go and get the bread for our family, the nice warm crusty loaf was an overwhelming temptation. It was always too long for the bag, and I couldn't resist the desire to 'trim it up' and then turn the loaf round in the bag. It was worth the slap when I got home.

Milk was usually delivered to the doors in Rillington Place by the local milkman early in the morning in glass bottles. There were no plastic containers then. That was when milk was milk and had cream on the top – not like the whitewash we have now! The full-cream milk had gold tops, and if you didn't bring it in, the birds, especially the blue tits, would peck holes in the lids to get to the cream. Some of the dairy companies used cardboard tops to protect the bottles.

'Uncle Reg' was amused to hear about the head teacher at my secondary school, Mr Markham. If he caned me, he used to leave lasting marks. 'I'm going to give you a choice,' Mr Markham always told his naughty pupils. 'I've got a thick cane that doesn't hurt too much, but lasts a long time. I've got a thin cane that hurts more but doesn't last so long. What is it to be?'

That entertained Christie. I also told him, as we munched on our cakes, that they thought I was undernourished at school. There was no one at home to cook for me, with Dad on night shifts and everyone else doing their own thing. Every morning the school used to give me a great big spoonful of cod liver oil and malt. A lot of people hated the stuff, but I quite liked it.

There was a science teacher who said to me: 'You're hungry, aren't you?'

'Yes, I am hungry, sir,' I answered.

There wasn't much food about after the war, and he would give me a shilling to buy something to eat. Next to the school was a pie and mash shop. So I would go and buy a pie and give him the change. He didn't need to do that for me, but he was a very kind man.

I traded stories with Christie, and he enjoyed hearing my tales from school. He had a good laugh as I had another run around the garden with Judy, chasing a ball.

Reg kept up to date with everything that was going on in the world. The year 1949 was a historically significant one during my school days, and I tried my best to keep up with current affairs. The key events I remember discussing with Christie were: the rationing of clothes ending in Britain; Éire becoming the Republic of Ireland and leaving the British Commonwealth; the Federal Republic of Germany being established; the People's Republic of China coming into being; the publishing of George Orwell's book Nineteen Eighty-Four; Legal Aid in England and Wales being introduced; and the Soviet Union testing its first atomic bomb. I probably tried to impress him with the topics we had discussed at school.

I enjoyed my conversations with Christie. I was young, and had no idea what he was like as a person behind closed doors, but his stories always interested me.

I could tell he was highly intelligent by the way he read the papers and finished crosswords. He was good with numbers, which explains why he had always done well in maths during his school years. He had been awarded a scholarship to Halifax Secondary

School, and I read later that his IQ was 128, which didn't surprise me at all. He seemed to know everything about everything. He had reached the highest rank in the Boy Scouts – a King's Scout – and was also a choirboy in the All Souls' Church Choir.

Reg told me more about his early life, including a little bit about his experiences in the First World War. He said he was a signalman and suffered badly after being gassed, and I believed him.

In later years, I checked his record to find out more. Christie enlisted with the Sherwood Foresters, Nottinghamshire and Derbyshire Regiment in 1916, aged 17. At that time he looked weedy, with light ginger hair – an ideal target for the Halifax bullies.

I believe he wanted to get away from Halifax, his harsh upbringing and those taunts about his sexual failures. In April 1918, he was seconded to the Duke of Wellington's Regiment during a major offensive by the Germans on the Western Front. A mustard gas shell exploded, rendering him unconscious. He said he was blind for five months and couldn't speak for more than three years, leaving him with his distinctive quiet, raspy voice.

The official records confirm he was disabled by gas. The gas must have burned Christie's throat, causing those voice problems in later life. I have no reason to doubt that he received the British War and Victory Medals he claimed to have been awarded for fighting in the trenches.

My own father had been gassed three times in the First World War. He was a sniper, and told me that the gas made his skin peel off. I often think that his lack of attention and care towards his own family may have come about because of the trauma of his wartime experiences. He never recovered fully from the anguish of being shot at and bombed while hungry, cold and wet, trying to survive up to his waist in mud.

Christie became a temporary postman in Halifax after the First World War. However, postal orders began to go missing from Halifax Post Office, and Christie turned out to be the culprit. Perhaps the pressures of the war skewed his mindset and led to him stealing the postal orders – I don't know. It was his first run-in with the law: he was arrested for the crime, and sent to Strangeways Prison in Manchester for three months.

Despite this early misdemeanour, he later rejoined the Post Office, working as a clerk at a savings bank in Shepherd's Bush. However, he was dismissed from that job, presumably because they found out about his previous offence.

It has been reported that Christie had some medical training prior to the Second World War. This is highly doubtful, and he certainly never showed me any books about medicine. Some claim that he showed Evans a first-aid book, offering to carry out an abortion on Beryl when she fell pregnant for a second time, but I don't believe a word of that. He never mentioned having trained to be a doctor.

'Uncle Reg' told me how he joined the police during the Second World War – still such a recent event back then. He applied to become a War Reserve Constable, and he was taken on as number 07732, based at Harrow Road. In wartime, it would have been easy for him to slip through the net despite having a criminal record, with thousands of men applying to join the force all at once. He was handed the full powers of a police officer, and was sworn in under the Special Constables Act of 1923.

Younger men went into the armed forces, while retired police officers and older people became War Reserve Constables. Christie's age and health conditions would hardly have made him first choice for the fighting overseas; also, after his experiences in the First World War, returning to the horrors of battle was the last thing he would have wanted.

'Uncle Reg' was tasked with ensuring that traffic flowed correctly. He actually made a complaint about cars parking in Rillington Place, as he wanted to keep that street clear of visitors. He seemed to want as few people hovering around his home as possible. His other roles included tracking down 'enemy aliens' and apprehending army deserters.

He received two commendations: one of them praised him for his investigations of bicycle theft, and on another occasion he was commended for arresting a man who was giving false air-raid warnings.

'I would make a good detective,' he told me. 'They should get me to help solve some of those murder cases.'

Reg Christie knew what to look for at a crime scene. He harboured further ambitions in the police, despite having a criminal record of his own. He told one of his colleagues that he would like to be a regular CID man, and what a thrill it would be to track down a murderer.

I wondered if officer Christie could have solved the case involving Vera Page, who lived only a few hundred yards from Rillington Place, in Blenheim Crescent. The case dates back to the early 1930s when Vera, aged 10, disappeared after visiting a relative. Her body was discovered in undergrowth in Addison Road, a couple of miles away. She had been raped and strangled. A labourer, Percy Orlando Rush, 41, was the prime suspect. There was not enough evidence to charge him, and the case remains unsolved even today.

Fellow officers became suspicious of Reg when he was observed chatting happily to prostitutes. One policeman was about to arrest a prostitute, when Christie claimed that the woman was his wife. There was no arrest, but his bemused colleagues, on learning that this was not true, wondered what was going on and why he had stepped in. They saw him making friends with prostitutes in the West End, turning a blind eye and no doubt taking full advantage of whatever the ladies of the night had to offer at special rates.

There were many bombed-out buildings in a perilous state in London, and Christie would go round with another officer, frequently finding bodies amongst the rubble. People who had been killed in the bombings were often still lying inside the houses. The police were also tasked with searching for vagrants who sought shelter in the unstable ruins.

Reserve Constable Christie acted officiously, holding up his warrant card and striding around proudly in his uniform. The sense of power he got from his status of a law enforcer went to his head. When he went on patrol, he was looking for any little offence that he could clamp down on.

During Christie's spell as a War Reserve Constable, Dr Odess was kept busy with Christie's ailments. Despite passing the police medical examination, which stated he was in good health, he took 180 days off during his service of four years and four months. Complaints included 'flu, chills and tonsillitis'. He also spent some time off sick after walking into a letterbox during the blackout and injuring his nose.

Bombs fell while he was on duty, and he had a couple of narrow escapes. A bomb in Harrow Road, near the police station, blew him off his feet. He told me he got up, ran to the scene and tended to the injured. Another time, he said, a gas main fractured in the street and he battled on with his work despite inhaling the fumes.

Reg told me he applied unsuccessfully to become an ARP (Air Raid Precautions) Warden, supervising the blackout in Paddington. He didn't say why he had been rejected, and I thought it better not to ask. ARP Wardens used to go from house to house checking people's curtains, and Christie did too, as part of his role with the police. If they saw a chink of light coming through your window, they would bang on your door and tell you to put the light out.

The blackout started just before hostilities began on 3 September 1939, when Britain and France declared war on Germany. Heavy blackout curtains were used, although people improvised with cardboard and paint, too. Before sunset, you had to cover your doors and windows completely, because German bombers looked for any chink of light to attack.

The headlights of vehicles had covers, deflecting the beam onto the ground. The same system was used for traffic lights. Street lights were switched off, or covered to point the beam towards the ground. The inside lights of buses had cowls over them to keep light to a minimum. It was a nightmare for conductors, who couldn't tell the difference between copper and silver coins during the blackout. Netting covered the bus windows to protect people from glass splinters when bombs fell.

Uncle Reg had many quirky stories to tell. He said men were advised to walk with their shirts hanging out, making them visible to drivers using dimmed headlights. He told me that people were urged to wear white clothes during the hours of darkness so that they could be seen by drivers. There were many more road accidents than usual because of the blackout. White stripes were even painted on lamp-posts and roads to improve safety.

Commercial opportunities arose for luminous accessories to be sold. There were customised handbags and plastic flowers that reflected light. Buttons received the same treatment, so that they glowed when you shone a light on them. The spivs of the time, always looking for easy money, had a field day.

Many falls were reported as people plunged down steps, bumped into phone boxes or tripped up on the pavement because they couldn't see. Christie, one of the casualties after his letterbox incident, remembered helping people who had fallen over on the pavement or lost their way in the dark.

The enforced blackout lasted until 23 April 1945, shortly after the liberation of Belsen concentration camp. Around 60,000 prisoners were discovered, starving and seriously ill, and the camp contained the bodies of 13,000 people. The Allies were closing in on Berlin and the threat of air attack on Britain was over.

Much of what I've read about Christie over the years is wide of the mark. He was a long and thin man, probably about 5ft 10in, or possibly slightly taller. He usually wore circular glasses and I was intrigued by the big bald dome of his head. He never looked well. He suffered from a variety of health complaints, including that painful back. He used to tell me his back was hurting, and he would hold it while he got up to make the tea or take the dishes away. I believe he also suffered from diarrhoea, headaches and piles, but naturally, he only ever mentioned to me that his back was painful. He was always going to see

Doctor Odess: his number of appointments between 1937 and 1952 totalled 174.

Books and articles sometimes refer to him as 'John' during his London years. When I was in and around Rillington Place, most people knew him as 'Mr Christie', but friends and family certainly still knew him by his middle name of 'Reg'.

Reg Christie had married Ethel Simpson on 10 May 1920, two years after the end of the First World War. They set up home in Sheffield, not far from where Reg had grown up in Halifax. In Sheffield, Christie's taste for the murky side of life became apparent, as he made frequent visits to prostitutes. Perhaps this inclination can be traced back to that humiliating sexual failure as a teenager, and his subsequent desire for control. He must have had some success in bed with Ethel, though, because she became pregnant. Sadly, however, Ethel suffered a miscarriage.

Reg and Ethel split up after a short time together, when Reg claimed she was having an affair. She was certainly an attractive young woman at the time, but there is no real evidence of an affair. He had brief spells as a painter, before landing a ground job with the RAF and moving to London in 1923.

Violence reared its ugly head again in 1928 when Christie moved in with Maude Cole and her son. Some say the woman was a prostitute, although there is no evidence of that. An argument flared up over Christie's lack of work and income, and he picked up a cricket bat and hit Maude over the head, causing her severe injuries. He later claimed that it was an accident, as he was just 'testing' the bat, but the magistrates didn't believe a word of it, branding him a coward and a liar. The attack was described as vicious and unprovoked, and led to six months' hard labour in Wandsworth Prison.

Reg Christie's conflict with law and order continued, and he was also jailed for stealing a car. Many writers have said that the car belonged to a priest, of all people, but it actually belonged to Christie's employer at the time.

Ethel visited her husband in prison while he was serving a sentence for the car theft. They had a chat about a reconciliation, and she decided to join him in London on his release.

In the middle of 1937, two years before the start of the Second World War, Reg and Ethel set up home at a new address. It would become one of the most infamous locations in the entire country. Initially, they occupied the top two rooms that were to become home for Evans and Beryl 11 years later. The Christies moved down to the ground floor in December 1938.

Reg and Ethel Christie's new address was 10 Rillington Place.

Chapter 3
Escaping the Bombs

My big sister was born Beryl Susanna Thorley on 19 September 1929. Next in our family came Basil William Clayton Thorley on 7 May 1931, followed by our sister Isabella Patricia Rose Thorley, known as Pat, on 10 March 1933. I completed the set on 22 August 1934, clocking in as Peter John Thorley. Our parents were William Clayton Thorley, born on 16 November 1888, and Elizabeth Thorley (née Simmonds), who was born on 10 January 1889.

Beryl, Basil, Pat and I were lucky to survive the Second World War. Shortly after hostilities broke out in 1939, we were sent away from London, along with thousands of other kids. We were worried about not seeing our mother, who was suffering from bronchial asthma, pleurisy and other debilitating conditions. We would see our parents only twice over the next three and a half years.

When Germany invaded Poland, the powers that be knew a massive operation had to be set in place. War was declared at the beginning of September 1939. I was still only five years old and, like all the other children, totally confused about leaving our loved ones behind. Hundreds of us from local schools waved goodbye to our parents and boarded fleets of buses.

Our parents packed bags for us. We all had one case to take with us, with just our essentials. These included night clothes, plimsolls or shoes to wear indoors, a change of underwear, spare socks and stockings, a comb, towel, toothbrush, handkerchiefs and face cloth. We brought coats with us, too, as autumn and winter were approaching. All of us had boxes containing our gas masks that we had to carry at all times. Those masks, when we wore them, made us look like monsters. We each had a small packet of food to eat on the journey, and we made sure we had our blue children's ration books with us.

We had labels pinned on our clothes, with our name and school. We weren't alone, because a party of teachers and volunteers were on the buses, too. They came up and down, chatting to us and looking out for children who seemed upset.

Hundreds of thousands of children were sent out to the countryside during those first three days of the evacuation. There were trains, buses and even ships setting off from the River Thames, heading to places like Lowestoft and Felixstowe on the coast.

The girls on our bus wore pretty dresses, while the boys wore everyday shorts and jumpers.

It was sad to start with – boarding those buses and heading off, not knowing where we were going, and confused about why we were leaving our parents behind. On the other hand, there was something exciting about boarding the big bus and going on an adventure. There were mixed emotions; we had no idea what was happening.

I sat beside Beryl near the back of the bus. She looked after me. Beryl was unusually quiet on the journey, probably because she knew we were heading off into the unknown. How could we be sure that we were going to be taken care of? Would there be no bombs, just because we were leaving London? All those thoughts must have filled Beryl's head as she gazed out of the bus window, holding my hand tightly and reassuring me that everything was going to be all right.

In the seats behind us, Pat and Basil chatted away. Beryl looked round occasionally to make sure her brother and sister were all right and opened the little window above their heads. I've no idea what they were talking about. I just heard them rabbiting on, with most of the noise coming from Basil.

Our destination was the picturesque village of Brockham in Surrey, and the journey didn't seem to take that long. We were used to built-up areas with lots of smoke and pollution, but suddenly we could see trees and fields everywhere. When we arrived in Brockham, there was a big green in the middle of the village.

We were taken to a building that may have been a school hall, where we were checked for lice. That was normal procedure at the time. After that, all our names were checked on a list and we were dropped off at our new homes.

We weren't all in the same house, and our little family group was broken up. Beryl, 10 years old, seemed destined for a charmed life: her new abode was the local sweet shop! It was run by a Mr and Mrs Howe. The shop was at one end of the green, opposite the church at the other. It was next to a pub called the Duke's Head, nowadays the Grumpy Mole. Beryl told us about her daily treats from the sweet shop – still rationed, of course – and she even smuggled out the odd morsel for the rest of us. She was content with her new surroundings, and would stay there for the whole duration of our evacuation.

Pat was sent to a Mrs Blunden, while Basil and I went to Mrs Smith in Chestnut Road. Seeing the name of the street, we hoped that there would be conkers to play with. Alas, we were surrounded only by edible chestnuts, and so the conker duels were put on hold.

Mrs Smith's accommodation was hardly five-star. We had to sleep in the kitchen cupboard under the stairs with a gas meter above our heads.

One night, we were shaken awake by the biggest, most almighty bang you could ever hear. It shook the house to its foundations.

We dashed out of the cupboard and peered out of a window to see what was going on. A bomb had made a direct hit on the house next door, and the building was a smouldering pile of rubble. Being so young, it was difficult to comprehend what was going on. The family living there must all have been killed. Nobody said if that had happened. I just prayed that no one was inside at the time.

Beryl and Pat, a few hundred yards away, heard the explosions. I ran through the village to tell them both we were all right, and we just hugged in the middle of the street. We were so young, and yet death threatened us at any moment.

It seemed we had jumped out of the frying pan into the fire. I learned later that Brockham was hit by 42 high explosives and more than 600 incendiary bombs during the war. A long string of bombs went up to the top of Box Hill in the village, lighting up the night sky. Presumably they were ditching the remainder of their payload after air raids elsewhere. I can't imagine that they had pinpointed an idyllic Surrey village for targeted attacks.

Another time I was walking home with Pat and one of our guardians in the pitch darkness. I had switched on my torch to lead the way, when suddenly I heard a plane overhead. I pointed my torch towards the heavens to try to catch sight of the aircraft. How stupid! It was a German bomber flying over the village. The pilot spotted the light and a bomb whizzed down in our direction. Fortunately, it fell in a nearby wood and we all escaped unscathed once more. I wasn't completely unscathed, of course, because I received a robust clump on the ear for my troubles.

Beryl wasn't with us on that occasion – she was at home at her sweet shop. When she heard from Pat about my stupidity with the torch, she gave me a mouthful at school the next day. I know I deserved every word of it.

Seven V1 flying bombs, or 'doodlebugs', fell in and around Brockham. When we heard the engine cut out, we knew the bomb was hurtling towards the ground, about to explode. Day after day, we escaped by the skin of our teeth.

We were surrounded by airfields, which were the target for many of the German air raids. Redhill was only six miles away. Spitfires were based there, with squadrons of Polish and Canadian pilots. The airfield played a key role in the large-scale attack on Dieppe in August 1942.

RAF Kenley was also nearby, and proved to be an important base for RAF Hurricanes. The Luftwaffe carried out extensive raids, all perilously close to our new homes in Brockham.

Sunday, 18 August 1940 was a lovely sunny day, but the peace of the Surrey countryside was shattered by fierce fighting. The Germans threw everything they had at Kenley, destroying more than sixty RAF fighter aircraft. The Luftwaffe lost 70 planes. The death toll was horrendous on both sides, with many service personnel and civilians killed and wounded on the ground too.

I don't remember seeing any actual dogfights around Brockham, but the skies were often full of aircraft going to or returning from missions. There were vapour trails leading up into the blue, so high up. Beryl told me how young and brave the pilots were. She understood that the people flying the Spitfires were in their teens, not really that much older than her, sacrificing their lives for our country.

I often wondered about the German air crews. Surely they couldn't all be bad men? I thought they couldn't help being born in Germany and called up to fight for their country. I didn't know what war was really all about, and was still too young to take it all in.

The London Blitz began on a Saturday afternoon, 7 September 1940. It followed a sustained assault on airfields and radar stations. Nearly 350 bombers as well as more than 600 fighters blackened the skies. Another raiding party arrived shortly afterwards to wreak even more havoc and try to break the morale of Londoners. There was destruction on a massive scale, but a defiant mood prevailed throughout the city.

Almost unbelievably, this sustained bombing campaign lasted for the next 57 days. There were horrific stories. A school being used as an air-raid shelter was hit, killing 450 people. The horizon was lined with hundreds of fires. More than 170,000 people sheltered in underground stations as the bombs rained down.

Beryl tried to reassure Basil, Pat and me that we were probably safer in Brockham than in London, because the capital was being targeted, whereas we were only being hit by stray bombs. After seeing all the damage in the village, we took some convincing!

We all had to carry gas masks, included with our belongings, or have them available at short notice. Because of all the gas used during the First World War, there were fears that perhaps the bombs being dropped now might have gas in them too.

The masks were frightening-looking things, so some of them were painted in bright, friendlier colours, and given the names of cartoon characters to make them more child-friendly. They were made of rubber, with round eyepieces made from plastic.

The mask was held on your head with straps. We had to push our chins into the mask and pull the straps over our heads. At the end of the mask was a filter with holes in it. The filter contained asbestos to absorb poisonous gases. It doesn't sound too healthy to us nowadays, knowing what we know about the dangers of asbestos and lung disease.

You could make a funny noise when you breathed out through the mask, like 'blowing a raspberry'. Beryl and I used to make that irritating sound for a laugh. We were taught to make a game of putting on the mask, and then the whole process didn't seem so terrifying.

I saw adults walking around with their masks in cardboard boxes over their shoulders. There was still a chance for ladies to look fashionable, though. Upper-class women had handbags with a compartment for a mask, which poked out at the bottom and almost blended into their outfits.

Basil and I were moved around quite a bit in the local area. We gained a reputation for being the 'terrible twins', as we got up to so many pranks. The difference in our ages was three years, but we looked very alike, and both of us enjoyed fooling around.

All the evacuee children attended school at the village hall in Brockham Green, three miles from where we were living. We had to walk there and back every day, although we were fit young lads and thought nothing of it, really. Pat and Beryl didn't have so far to go, fortunately for them. Beryl only had to cross the green from the sweet shop. The village hall school had one classroom, one teacher and about 25 kids. Lessons were standard for the time: reading, writing and arithmetic.

'You two are fooling around too much,' Beryl scolded me and Basil after school one day. 'Don't you know there's a war on? It's no time to be playing jokes. Let's just find our way through this and get home safely to Mum and Dad.' She would have known that we paid little attention to the best advice.

Just as we were settling into our lessons, the school closed. Oh, goodie, no more school! Or so we thought. Wrong.

We were all sent to the local Roman Catholic school, an extra mile down the road. It was a convent, really. Anyone found misbehaving could expect a hearty slap on the top of the leg from one of the friendly nuns.

We moved to another house in Chestnut Road, ruled by a Mrs Mackrell. She got more and more upset by Basil's strange habit:

he sniffed everything, and I mean everything. When we went to church, he even sniffed the hymn books, and seemed to enjoy that horrible old musty smell. He sniffed his clothes, my clothes and everybody's clothes. If he was in a room, he would look around for things to sniff. I've no idea where he got that habit, and I stayed clear of him if he started sniffing.

One day Mrs Mackrell was serving breakfast, and Basil decided to put his nose too close to his porridge. She glared and glared at Basil, who just smiled and decided to have yet another sniff.

'That's it, I've had enough!' she yelled at him, pushing his face down into the plate of porridge. 'Sniff, sniff, sniff. All you do is sniff. Why do you have to sniff everything?'

'Take that,' Basil replied with a snarl, hurling the plateful of porridge in the direction of our upset hostess. 'I can sniff if I want to.'

'Right, you two are out! Get out of here now!'

We were gone that day, and other local families took their turns at looking after the 'terrible twins'. Another lady who regretted taking us in was Mrs Skinner, who lived at Council Cottages.

'She must be collecting kids,' I whispered to Basil when we were inside her little cottage. 'Looks like it's standing room only.'

It was a crush. There were children everywhere, standing and sitting, lying down or playing outside. We just had to make the best of it and find a corner to ourselves. We slept anywhere we could.

Our stay with Mrs Skinner was quite short. I seemed to get blamed for everything that went wrong.

Mrs Skinner's daughter Amy opened a drawer on a dressing table and stood on it like a step. Everything came crashing to the floor: ornaments, brushes, jewellery and a collection of trinkets. Unfortunately, the mirror came crashing down too and exploded into thousands of little pieces. Our landlady came back from the pub, slightly the worse for wear and not in the best of moods.

'It was Peter!' Amy hissed. 'He stood on the drawer like a step and everything fell off.'

I was not guilty, but who was going to believe me? Mrs Skinner picked up a stick and really let me have it on the legs. I was sore for days afterwards, and sorer because I was completely innocent…

Mrs Skinner was never very kind to us, and spoke to children in harsh tones. The farmers in Brockham used to feed their cows with white cabbages, and Mrs Skinner would bark: 'Go out into the field now and get me a cabbage. And pick some mushrooms while you're out there.'

One day we were waiting to cross the road and I wanted to go to the toilet, but a convoy was coming. It was a very slow convoy, with dozens of vehicles. The convoy seemed to go on forever and, still being small, I lost control and wet myself. I don't know what possessed me. There was a field behind and I could have gone there for a pee. When I got inside the house, Mrs Skinner gave me a clout across the ear. Basil didn't escape punishment either: subsequent enquiries revealed that I had crapped myself as well, and Mrs Skinner made Basil wash my pants!

Mrs Skinner ordered me to go upstairs and wash myself. I was only five years old, and I had to do this standing in the bath with the cold water running. The problem was, I had no flannel. I managed to reach for one on the side of the bath, which apparently belonged to Amy. When I had finished, I folded it neatly in half and replaced it on the side. I saw a towel, too, and used that to dry myself off. When the soiled cloth and discoloured towel were discovered by Amy, I received a firm clip over the other ear from her disgusted mother.

Once Mrs Skinner had had enough of us, our next stop was a cottage at the bottom of Box Hill with a Mrs Anderson. It was a house standing on its own beside the railway line. When a train went through in the early hours, loaded with tanks and ammunition, everything rolled off tables and shelves. The house actually shook. Adding to that, army convoys were on the move all the time, so sleep was a precious commodity. We didn't get much of it.

The final move for me and Basil came shortly afterwards, when we joined our sister Pat at Mrs Blunden's house. We slept in a so-called Anderson Shelter, made of corrugated iron in the garden and no relation to the previous family! We could hear planes going overhead, but fortunately we weren't attacked; I kept my torch well out of sight.

This was probably the happiest and most comfortable time of all – at least until Pat dropped one of Mrs Blunden's prize geraniums out the window. It was Pat's job to put the flowers out in the morning and bring them in at night. Pat was forgiven, although the 'terrible twins' tried more tricks on poor Mrs Blunden, despite repeated warnings from Beryl.

In 1943, Beryl, Basil, Pat and I all returned to our parents at 112d Cambridge Gardens, because the German bombing campaign had eased up a bit. When we returned to London, we were utterly astonished by the sight before our eyes. Our home city was like the face of the moon. There were craters everywhere, bombed-out houses and all sorts of wreckage piled up in the streets. Children were running round the craters, collecting shrapnel, as the shell fragments had become something of a currency among the kids.

A cinema in Edgware Road near Marble Arch was showing many of the new releases so we tended to go there as a family rather than to the Royalty. It was only a couple of miles on the bus, although that journey could be hazardous. Beryl to the rescue!

I remember one day we got on the 52 bus to go to Edgware Road and the smog was incredibly thick. There was so much pollution being pumped into the air from factories and coal fires, and this all combined with water particles, creating the poisonous fog. It was really horrible and you could hardly breathe. There was a bloke walking in front of our bus with a lamp so that the driver could crawl through the thick blanket of smog.

I looked out the window and all I could see was a horrible thick yellowish mass of muck. In those days they called it a 'pea souper'; it looked nearly as bad as the 'Great Smog of London' that killed thousands of people in 1952.

'We'll get there all right,' Beryl assured me as we sat next to each other near the front of the bus. 'When we get out, try to hold your breath a bit until we get into the cinema.'

I did feel happier with Beryl sitting next to me, as she was the oldest and I was the youngest child. I would have been about 10 and she would have been 15; the perfect older sister. As usual, she looked out for me and tried to make sure I was doing all the right things.

When we arrived in Edgware Road and went into the cinema, nothing much had changed. Because the doors were open, the building filled with smoke. People inside were smoking, too, so we couldn't see the screen, it was that bad. I remember a horrible choky feeling at the back of my throat, and it lasted for days.

We endured the film, although I can't remember what was showing. When we got out of the cinema, the smog was still just as bad, and you couldn't see your hand in front of your face. People had to be careful not to walk into lamp-posts or letter boxes. The bloke with the lamp was there again to guide the bus home, very slowly, through that choking muck, and it was not a night out with fond memories.

Another distinct wartime memory I must mention was the amount allowed for bathwater. It could never be more than six inches, usually poured into a small tin bath. You did what you were told in the war. If it had to be six inches, it was six inches. Beryl, the eldest, was first in and enjoyed the clean water.

The thought crossed our minds: what if someone was sent round to check the depth of the water? The older Basil wondered about displacement, with a higher water line because of someone in the tub. Would they bring a dipstick? We chuckled at the six inches regulation. Beryl and Pat could never understand how a lady was supposed to make do with six inches of water.

When the four of us were together I would always have the last dip, being the youngest. That meant I came out dirtier than when I went in. The water would then be poured out to clean the yard or whatever. Fortunately, they never threw the baby out with the bathwater.

At Christmas, we made the most of what we had. There wasn't much room at Cambridge Gardens. Grandma and Aunty Fay stayed with us for some time, so they had a little bedroom at the back, while Basil and I slept on a sofa in the front room. Beryl and Pat slept on a small bed in my mother's room. Dad was never there in the evenings because of his night shifts. Dad was working for the London Passenger Transport Board.

The film *Holiday Inn* came out with Bing Crosby singing *White Christmas*, as he sat at the piano performing a duet with Marjorie Reynolds. He also performed a little whistle during the song. Beryl used to drive us crackers by singing that song and whistling at Christmas. All over the house, wherever she was, she would sing it.

'For Christ's sake, Beryl, shut up!' we'd all say.

Every Christmas I think of Beryl singing, and it brings tears to my eyes. Lovely as Beryl was, she sang out of tune and I remember my dad putting his hands over his ears. Even worse, she couldn't whistle, but tried to impersonate Bing Crosby nonetheless. Beryl's attempt sounded like one of those old kettles howling on the stove. We loved her all the same.

Everyone gave each other a present, but it was never much. Beryl might get me crayons and I would wrap up a handkerchief as a present for her. If I saved up, I might have a small amount of chocolate for her. There was no money around, with rationing firmly in force, so it was the best we could do. Christmas stockings didn't have much in them – perhaps an apple or two.

As for Christmas lunch, we would save up coupons to buy a chicken or maybe a small cut of beef. Crackers were a rarity. Having said all of that, we usually enjoyed a homely, happy festive season, despite Beryl's constant renditions of *White Christmas*.

How I would miss my Beryl, Christmas after Christmas, in the years to come.

Chapter 4
Making a Meal of It

Our lives during and after the war often revolved around finding enough food to eat and making the most of what we were allowed.

Rationing was very strict. If you had sugar in your tea, you couldn't have jam on your bread. It was one or the other. Even today, I have jam on my bread because I don't have sugar in my tea. We had about two ounces of butter and a small amount of lard per person each week. You had a certain number of ration coupons to use up in a month, and you had to register with a grocer. People couldn't just walk in off the street and buy essentials.

A luxury like a leg of lamb would take up a lot of coupons, so treats like that normally had to be avoided. There were clothing coupons, and all confectionery was rationed, as our Beryl found out in her sweet shop. One month we could get half a pound of sweets, the next we might get a pound of them, and the month after that only get four ounces.

It was always my job to go to the shop with our ration books and hand over the sweet coupons. In London I would take the four sets of coupons to the local shop, where the sweets were weighed and put into four bags. On the way home I would carefully open the other three bags, take one or two sweets out from the others' rations, and suck them as hard as I could to get rid of the evidence.

Beryl, the oldest and the smartest, was suspicious that I had been thieving my siblings' sweets, noticing my poor effort to reseal the bags.

'Spit them out!' she ordered, as the others looked inside their bags.

When they realised what had happened, all three of them pounced on me, squeezed my mouth and tried to get me to eject the sweets as punishment. I eventually had to give up on my scheme and bring back their bags unopened.

While we were in Brockham, I had tried the same ruse with Pat and Basil, although Beryl sorted herself out with coupons, as she lived in the sweet shop.

Rationing was a gradual process as more items were added to the list. From 1940 the government limited bacon, butter, milk, sweets, meat, margarine, tea, jam, rice, dried fruit and soap. Even children had their own ration books. I remember, though, that we received extra allowances and always seemed to have enough milk and other staple foods. Bread was never rationed until after the war, when the demand for wheat outstripped supply.

Even coal was rationed because of the number of miners who had been called up for war service. We would see people chopping up fallen branches, in parks or wherever they could find them, to use for fuel.

People's lawns and flower beds became vegetable gardens. There was no rationing on fruit and vegetables, and occasionally I saw an orange from overseas, although I don't remember spotting any melons or exotic fruits until after the war.

Pigs and chickens also appeared outside houses in back yards and gardens, as Londoners found ways of compensating for the limitations in shops.

Fish and chip shops were still open. There was no rationing on fish, although supplies became short because of the dangers faced at sea by fishing crews. The fish was good enough, but often spoiled because the quality of the fat was low, resulting in a funny taste. Unless you could find a way round it, each person was allowed just one egg a week.

A 'utility clothing' scheme was brought in during 1941 to help the war effort and make the best use of resources. The import and manufacture of raw materials was controlled by the government, who were responsible for supplying cloth to companies.

There was a limit as to how much cloth manufacturers could use, so fewer items of clothing had pockets. Double-breasted suits became single-breasted. There was a ban on making trousers with turn-ups, so gentlemen bought trousers that were too long and asked their wives to make the turn-ups instead.

The surprise for consumers was that the quality still appeared quite high; manufacturers tried to add flair to their designs, so wartime outfits weren't all drab and devoid of fashion. Different colours started to appear, and leading fashion designers including Norman Hartnell and Hardy Amies were brought in to add some imagination.

For the ladies, like Beryl and Pat, there was a bonus: elastic was in short supply, but knickers were permitted to contain that vital ingredient.

As people continued to grow their own produce, the 'Dig for Victory' campaign was launched. You could eat as much as you liked from your own garden. And you could have as much beer as you wanted in the pubs until they ran out and the dray horses returned with more supplies.

Most of what we ate was local and seasonal, but one day I came face to face with a banana, and I thought it was a weird-looking thing. Beryl, up to her usual nonsense, must have got it from our cousin Moray, a greengrocer, or maybe from one of the American soldiers who were stationed around and about. In any case, we were at home in Cambridge Gardens and she held it up in front of me.

'Would you like one of these?' She laughed.

'What is it? Are you sure I can eat it?'

'Yes, it's a banana. Here, have a try.'

So I took hold of this long bendy yellow thing, and was about to put it in my mouth.

'No, not the skin. Not the skin!'

I had no idea what it was until she told me. I peeled off the skin and enjoyed the ripe fruit. And that was my first ever banana.

At home it was usually Beryl's job to butter the bread; how annoying was she? Beryl only buttered the bread in the middle, so the rest of it was dry. I tried to persuade her to spread everything thinly, so that the taste went all over the sandwich. She ignored me and persisted in filling up the middle!

The German planes were back in force in 1944, raining thousands of bombs on London again. We used to see the Spitfires go after the aircraft, illuminated in the searchlights. Beryl, Basil and I watched this happening during the daytime, too. We saw bombers being hit and plunging to the ground with smoke pouring from them. I'm sure we must have suffered losses, too. I just remember those brave Spitfire pilots weaving in and out of the bombers and shooting them down.

I was almost finished off by a Doodlebug, the V1 flying bomb. I was standing at the back door in Cambridge Gardens watching one come over. The engine cut out and I suddenly thought, Oh my God, where is that going to come down? Those flying bombs landed quickly when the engine cut out – they were heavy things.

I heard a loud bang and was blown down the passageway of the house. 112d Cambridge Gardens used to be a doctor's surgery, so there were no carpets. There were tiles in the passageway and I was swept right along by the blast. The flying bomb had crashed into the local church. The church was hit three times in total during the war, and we were very close by.

With all of this going on, our parents thought it safer to send London children out of the capital again. Pat stayed in Margate, while Basil and I were sent to a family at Aberystwyth in Wales. It was boring there, and we joked with each other that we would have had more fun dodging the bombs in London!

Having left school, Beryl, 15 years old by this time, decided to stay in London and learn shorthand and typing. She found an assortment of part-time work to pay for her tuition. One job saw her selling 'posh hats' in a high-class ladieswear shop at the top of Cambridge Gardens, only minutes away from home.

Over the following months, our mother's health deteriorated rapidly, not helped by the terrible air quality from the infamous London smog. If Beryl wasn't working she would be at home, sitting with our mum. There would always be one of the family with her, especially when Dad was working nights on the buses. I would take my turn to sit with Mum. She couldn't go into the air raid shelter outside, because people used to sit in there smoking and it wasn't good for her, so we had to stay indoors. The pressure of seeing the family through the war years had really taken its toll on her.

A couple of years after the end of the war, Mum was moved into hospital, where she passed away on 2 March 1947, aged only 52 years. She left our father with a young family of four children to look after. She was buried in accordance with Jewish tradition two days later. I attended with Basil and our father, who was not Jewish but was permitted to come.

On the day of Mum's funeral, both Basil and I were taken aside by our uncle, Monty Ellis from Mum's side of the family. He was there with my Aunty Nancy. Monty had a Rolls Royce. Nancy stayed in the car during the funeral, because it was really an all-male affair. Beryl and Pat didn't attend, as they knew the service would be dominated by the men.

Uncle Monty had a successful, long-established family business in London. The Ellis Brothers imported fancy mirrors and hairbrushes for dressing tables from Japan and the Far East. He had a large warehouse, which had been bombed during the war. However, Monty was paid out by the insurance and carried on without batting an eyelid. Uncle Monty and Aunty Nancy lived in an impressive property in St John's Wood.

'Listen boys, would you like to come and live as part of our family? You could get involved in the business and have more of a future. Maybe there's not much of a future for you where you are.'

Uncle Monty was right. It was a tremendous opportunity, although Basil couldn't quite see it. He was older than me, hot-headed, and knew his own mind, even if he was totally wrong and misguided.

'No thanks,' he told Uncle Monty, with a touch of rudeness in his voice. 'We're staying with Dad.'

I regretted missing that opportunity for the rest of my life. Perhaps if I had taken it, I might never have been sent to New Zealand two years later.

Beryl and Evans outside Mrs Probert's House in St Mark's Road.

Chapter 5

An Untrustworthy Man

Timothy John Evans entered the world on 20 November 1924.

His mother, Thomasina Agnes Lynch, was born in Merthyr Tydfil, Wales, in 1901. She married Daniel Evans when she was 21 years old. Her first child, a daughter, had been born in 1921; she was named Eleanor, often referred to as Eileen.

When Thomasina was pregnant with Timothy, her husband deserted her.

A few years later Thomasina met Penry Probert, who already had a son. They had a daughter together, born in September 1929. They called her Mary, and she was usually known as Maureen. Penry and Thomasina married four years later in 1933.

Work was hard to find in Wales, and in 1936, the family moved to London. Timothy Evans attended a school in Kensington. He wasn't an easy child, prone to temper tantrums. Later that year, he returned to Merthyr and was looked after by his grandmother.

By all accounts, he was a bit of a handful. Mrs Probert said that he used to kick and scream. If he didn't want to do something, there was no way of making him fall into line. He was known to bite his nails from a young age.

At school, he played football and enjoyed boxing, too, despite his foot injury. He was described as a poor scholar who lacked application, although he was often absent because of his foot problem. He was sent to a variety of places for treatment, including The Princess Louise Hospital in Kensington and the nearby St Charles' Hospital.

He left school at 13, still struggling to write his own name. He could barely read, and comics were his level of literacy, really. His IQ was in the range of 65 to 75 – much lower than Reg Christie's intelligence. Physically, he grew to about 5ft 6in and was always hampered by a permanent limp from a swimming accident.

He was probably close to being mentally retarded, as they would have described the condition then; nowadays, he would have been classed as having an intellectual disability. There have been reports of mental illness in the family, and perhaps this had an impact on Timothy further down the line. His grandfather had a reputation as a wife-beater; Timothy certainly inherited some characteristics there.

At the age of 14 he rejoined his family in Notting Hill, where he worked for a short time as a van boy. He also carried out some jobs as a painter and decorator. He then returned to Glamorganshire, where he worked in the mines, earning 10s. 4d. a week. That job didn't last long either, because of his bad leg, and back to London he went. He took on a variety of other work, but nothing lasted. His health problems prevented him from carrying out National Service, although it is recorded that he was in the Home Guard and worked as a Civil Defence messenger.

Timothy Evans was a compulsive liar, who frankly would not recognise the truth if it jumped up and bit him. On top of this, he could fabricate the most outrageous stories – such as the time when he told Christie his father was an Italian Count. He was notorious for bragging among everyone who knew him, including his own family. In fact, because of this, he was regarded as something of a source of entertainment, particularly in the public houses he frequented. Even his mother is known to have said that her son had a vivid imagination and was a terrible liar. It was said of him that he would lie for 'financial gain'.

Tim had his first sexual experience with a girlfriend when he was about 18. The relationship didn't last long, though, and his girlfriend told him it was over. From 1942 until his marriage to Beryl, he frequently resorted to prostitutes, alongside his other main extravagances of drinking to excess, and gambling.

His stepfather is purported to have said that Timothy Evans had a violent temper and got into bad company when he left school. His mother didn't deny this, but could not believe he was a man who would use actual physical violence. His half-sister Maureen also had to agree that Evans was a bit rough with his temper.

Trouble was never far away. On 25 April 1946, Evans appeared before West London Magistrates, charged with stealing a car and driving it without a licence or insurance. He was convicted as a petty criminal and fined 60 shillings.

He ran into further problems over stolen goods. When questioned about a stolen rug and briefcase, he claimed he had got them from Beryl's friends Charles and Joan Vincent, of Westbourne Park Road. This was nonsense: the Vincents were highly respectable people. It soon transpired that the goods were taken from another gentleman living at the same address. Evans had a reputation for selling stolen watches, and he certainly lived up to it.

When I met Evans for the first time after the blind date, I couldn't help wondering what our Beryl was doing with him. To me, she seemed far too good for him. I suppose she just needed some sort of security going forward.

Timothy was short, only marginally taller than Beryl. He drank and smoked to excess, he gambled, he bragged, and he lied non-stop. He was always saying 'I bet you' that this or that would happen – it was a tedious catchphrase of his.

One of his favourite watering holes was a pub called the Elgin, not far from the KPH bar. On his way home from work, he would have two or three pints in one of those places. When he went out later, he could knock back another six or seven. I don't know where he put it all.

In the bars, he would talk about Queens Park Rangers football club and their latest results. He was probably putting bets on their matches, as he often did on horse races, which he was addicted to. The dog-racing track at White City wasn't far away, and he also kept a close eye on that.

He had a reputation in the bars for borrowing money, and people soon got wise to him. He would ask for a few shillings, and said he would repay them the next day when he'd been paid. The regulars soon realised that nobody ever got their money back from Timothy Evans the next day, so lending to him soon became an absolute no-no. One of his employers gave him a loan to tide him over, and the money was never repaid.

I gave Beryl money if I had any. Despite my young age, I felt desperately sorry for her and was keen to help in any way I could. But I would never lend to her brutal other half.

Did I trust Timothy Evans?

Not a chance.

Chapter 6
A New Life by the Seaside

In 1948, out of the blue, Dad said he wanted to take Patricia, Basil and me to Brighton for the day. Beryl had married Timothy Evans and was soon to move into 10 Rillington Place; Pat was spending some time at home with us again after her stay in Margate.

Dad's behaviour, after Mum's death in 1947, had seemed so out of character; we wondered what he was up to. We set off for Victoria Station, caught the train, and were quite looking forward to a day out. But we were in for a shock. During the journey, Dad explained that we would be moving to Brighton to live quite soon, once he had finalised matters at Cambridge Gardens.

There was another even greater shock in store. Dad said he wanted to introduce us to a 'lady friend' of his called Marguerita. We soon learned that she lived in Brighton, where she worked as a chambermaid in a hotel. Well, we imagined a ride in a chugging steam train and a day out at the seaside, so it wasn't all bad.

When we arrived at Brighton, Dad told us that Marguerita was going to meet us at the station. We were intrigued. We were mucky young teenage boys, imagining a beautiful lady on the coast in Brighton. A vision of blonde loveliness approached and smiled at us sweetly. We looked at each other, wide-eyed. She kept walking.

We felt a little downcast until we heard our father exclaim, 'Here she is!' Suddenly the earth shook, as a peculiar shape thundered down the platform and stood sternly before us.

Our gasps of disappointment must have echoed round Brighton Station. Pat was rooted to the spot, while Basil and I jumped back on the nearest train, hoping to escape. The train wasn't going anywhere. Marguerita prised us from the safe haven of the train carriage and carted us off to the Regent Restaurant for afternoon tea. We would have much preferred the Peter Pan kids' area on the beach.

Returning home, the reality of the day's events began to sink in. For me, the thought of leaving Beryl in London on her own, not knowing how often I would see her, was devastating. She was about to move into her first proper home, with a newborn baby to look after, and her family were deserting her. To make matters worse, her husband was someone I really detested.

Basil was older than me and seemed to be more than happy where he was. He had his own circle of friends and a job, and decided that he wasn't going to move to Brighton. Pat was resigned to living with her father. Like her, I had little choice.

Dad worked quickly to relinquish his tenancy at Cambridge Gardens, so our grandmother and aunt, who shared the flat, had to make alternative arrangements without delay. It appeared to us that he had already committed himself to rented accommodation at 10 Chapel Street, Brighton.

And so we moved down to Sussex in February 1948.

That move came far sooner than expected. Once again, Pat and I were taken out of our comfort zones. After all, it was only a short while since the death of our mother.

I kept thinking about how I would manage to see Beryl in an environment where I knew she was going to be unhappy. Yes, she had a baby on the way and all seemed fine on the surface. But I had seen how Evans spoke to her and how much he drank, and was really concerned.

I couldn't stop thinking about how much I was going to miss her. I made up my mind to get a paper round. That way, I would make enough money to see her at least once a week.

For a short while, until finishing school, I attended St John the Baptist Roman Catholic School in Brighton. It was far removed from Solomon Wolfson Jewish School, where I had studied in Kensington. Naturally, I was excused morning assemblies on religious grounds. So that I should not become idle, I was delegated to the duties of 'toilet cleaning' by Sister Augustus.

I wasted no time in getting the paper round and, as soon as I had saved enough money, I visited Beryl and Geraldine regularly.

When I left school at 14, I found myself a job at the Old Ship Hotel on Brighton seafront as a page boy. I received £4 10s per week, from which I gave Dad £2 10s towards the family housekeeping. Fortunately, I was able to have my meals at the hotel while on duty, and made quite a bit extra in tips.

It wasn't long before Marguerita moved in. We were expected to call her 'Mum'. We decided that we would never class her as that, not ever, but agreed we would call her Margaret to her face, and 'Monkey Glands' in her absence. It didn't take her long to make it perfectly clear that she hated having kids around. She regarded us as an encumbrance and intrusion in her life.

When Dad eventually told me I was going to New Zealand, the only benefit I could see was an escape from Marguerita's catering skills.

She would go to the greengrocer and buy the biggest cabbage she could find and take it home, ready to prepare for dinner. When it came to cooking the cabbage, she would take it out of the bag and place it whole, caterpillars included, into a large saucepan. She would fill the pan with cold water and boil the poor veg until it was stewed and turned a delicate shade of yellow. Then it was served alongside whatever other horrors she had concocted. The saving grace was the pie shop on the corner of the road less than two minutes away.

Beryl was suddenly far away, in a dangerous place, and we would never get her back.

Tim Evans, Eileen holding Geraldine, and Beryl.

Chapter 7
The Ring of Truth

The thought of not seeing my beloved Beryl for such a long time played on my mind. I was really fond of Geraldine, too, and knew I would miss them both terribly. Why on earth did I have to go to New Zealand, of all places? It sounded bonkers to me.

I received a letter with my departure date: I had to report to Tilbury Docks early on Saturday, 5 November 1949, to board SS Rimutaka for the 16,000-mile voyage to New Zealand. I would be one of more than 800 passengers.

Before I left, I had to see Beryl and Geraldine to break the news in person and say a proper farewell. I decided to travel by train from Brighton to London to see them on Wednesday, 2 November, three days before my departure.

As soon as I arrived at Rillington Place, I sensed something was wrong. It was just instinct. I knocked at the door and Christie answered, as usual. He smiled and gestured for me to come inside. He had on his usual shirt and tie with pressed trousers and shiny shoes.

'Off you go upstairs,' he whispered in that soft voice of his, seeing how keen I was to visit my sister and little Geraldine.

At the top of the stairs there was a landing, with Beryl and Timothy's kitchen door on the left. The kitchen window looked out onto the back garden. The table in Beryl's kitchen was a sizeable wooden one, and could be used not only for mealtimes but for the preparation of food generally. She was always scrubbing it clean. It helped that the table was dual purpose, because the rooms were quite small and couldn't accommodate much furniture. They never used a tablecloth. Due to the sloping foundations of the property, if you put an egg on the kitchen table, it would roll straight off the other end.

To the right of the landing, there was a door to the bedroom and lounge area. There was no carpet, but light-coloured linoleum covered the floor. It was just after the war, and people didn't have much money for home comforts. The bedroom and lounge area were at the front of the house, overlooking the street. Beryl answered the door to the right, and her dark brown eyes looked so sad. It looked to me as if she was really frightened and had been crying. I knew the relationship was in trouble although, being so young, I hoped they would patch things up and get some professional help for Evans's drinking and violence.

Downstairs, workers were coming and going in and out of the front door and through to the wash house at the back. They were walking through the passage past Christie's front room with tools and planks of wood.

I asked Beryl why the workers were there. She told me that Christie had complained about a blocked drain, reporting to Kensington Borough Council that there was a bad smell coming out and investigations were needed.

After an inspection by the council, it was decided that remedial works were required. The drain needed attention, and damp was also affecting the property. The landlord's agents had been served with a notice advising them of the defects and saying repairs were necessary.

The roof of the front room bay window on the ground floor was in desperate need of attention, with rising damp in the external wall. The floor in the ground-floor passage was in a dangerous condition. The yard water closet had some issues, too: defective plaster on the walls and the roof in dangerous condition. The report said that the 'ground-floor back addition room' needed repairs because of dampness in the walls; I knew that area as the wash house.

The agents of the landlord were Messrs Martin East, who gave instructions to Larter and Sons of Holland Park. The men who carried out the work were plasterer Frederick Willis, plasterer's mate Frederick Jones and carpenter Robert

Anderson. They were all under the supervision of their manager, Raymond Phillips. I could see them loading and unloading materials from their van.

The workers had been due to start on Monday, 31 October, a couple of days before my visit. However, there was no chance of roofing work being done, because of heavy rain in the preceding days, and they were sent elsewhere to carry out indoor jobs.

I was well away from the workmen while I chatted to Beryl upstairs in her flat over a cup of tea.

'He's been gambling again.' My sweet sister sighed. 'He took everything to make a bet and go drinking last night. We're getting into even more debt with all his drinking and gambling. We're behind with the payments as usual for furniture and everything. What am I going to do, Peter? I know now that this marriage has been such a mistake. A disaster.'

I knew that we were free to talk, as Evans was out driving his delivery van before the regular pub stop on the way home.

'What else is he doing?' I asked hesitantly. 'Is he still hitting you? I can see the marks.'

'Nothing's changed.' She sobbed. 'Most nights he comes home drunk after the pubs have closed and starts a row. It turns into a fight and, yes, he's still knocking me about.'

I felt so, so angry. How could he attack a kind, beautiful lady like this? What about Geraldine in her cot? Was this really a safe environment for a baby? The little one would see what was going on. I was horrified, but there was worse to come. There was no way I could have prepared myself for what she was about to say.

'And Tim said he would kill me. Whether he means it or not, I don't know.'

I froze, trying to take in what she had said.

'Is he totally mad? He won't kill you. Maybe he was just drunk and didn't realise what he was saying. Although that's no excuse.'

'Oh yes, he knew what he was saying all right.' Beryl sighed, with a calmness that sent shivers down my spine. 'And he meant it. I could see the hate in his eyes, drink or no drink. I'm really frightened of him, Peter. I wish I was going back to Brighton with you and taking Geraldine there. I don't feel safe here at all.'

'Look, I'll discuss this with Dad when I get back and hope he can do something,' I said. My uncaring father still had not stepped up to the plate, but I was determined to make him listen. 'It sounds dangerous living here. You and Geraldine don't deserve this sort of existence.'

I hadn't yet told Beryl about my upcoming journey to the other side of the world. It was far from the ideal situation, with my sister so desperately in need of my help. Now it seemed even her life might be at risk. I thought the best I could do for the moment would be to try to ease the financial crisis.

'You say you've no money at all? I hear he has plenty of cash to throw around in the pub. He should be spending it on you and Geraldine, I can see that.'

'No, Peter, I don't have any money,' Beryl cried. 'I can't get any food or milk for the baby.'

I was deeply upset. Beryl never owed anyone anything; she always paid her way. Before moving to Brighton, we had lived nearby in Cambridge Gardens as a family, and she always made sure she did more than her fair share of the housekeeping. This lack of money was totally alien to her careful nature. Evans was squandering everything they had, and she was powerless to stop him.

I emptied my pockets and counted out 10 shillings. That is only equivalent to 50 pence now, but was worth a lot more back then. I already had my train ticket to Brighton and enough change for my bus fare back to Victoria. As I handed over the money, Beryl wept with gratitude.

I looked round and saw Geraldine bouncing up and down in her cot without a care in the world, bless her. Geraldine was always pleased to see me. She was a chunky, happy little soul, jumping up and down there in her pink romper suit with a cheeky smile on her face. Beryl continued to cry and I gave her a big, big hug.

'Hang on, I'm going up to the corner shop to get you some things,' I told her. 'Just sit there and I'll be back in a few minutes.'

I went out of the front door and set off to the right along Rillington Place. It wasn't far; there weren't many houses in the street. I walked under the railway bridge across Rillington Place, and at the end of the street I turned left into St Mark's Road.

The shop was just a few yards down St Mark's Road, beside the red phone box. That traditional red box, with a heavy old-fashioned black phone and dial, was a landmark beside the corner shop. It was the same phone box Beryl had used to call the police the previous month.

It was a handy little shop for the usual household supplies – milk, newspapers, sweets and all that. It was run by one old man, all alone – at least, he seemed old to me, as I was still only a young lad. He was friendly enough and gave me what I needed to cheer up Beryl. I didn't have ration coupons with me, which were still needed to buy supplies in those post-war years, but I must have looked in need, because he let me buy a few groceries for her. Bread was in short supply, but he gave me a loaf along with a couple of pints of milk, plus a few other bits.

I raced back with the provisions, through the front door and up the stairs as quickly as I could. As I went into the bedroom, I saw Geraldine jumping up and down in her cot as usual, full of energy. Beryl started preparing some food for Geraldine straight away, and I knew I needed to let her know about my impending trip.

'Beryl, I need to tell you something. I know it's going to be a surprise to you, and it was a shock to me. But it's something I wanted to tell you in person. I've been trying to get out of it, but I can't. I wasn't expecting to find you in all this trouble.'

'Get out of what?'

'I'm going to New Zealand,' I sort of mumbled, trying to get the words out.

'New Zealand? Do tell me you're joking.'

'I know, it's on the other side of the world, and you're in all this trouble, too.'

'Peter, why on earth are you going there? You're only 14, for goodness sake.'

'It's some sort of emigration scheme. Dad told me. I think his new woman wants me out of the way. I'm dreading it. I'm actually leaving on Saturday.'

'Oh my God, Peter. I would never have believed that Dad would do such a thing!'

'Well, we'll keep in touch and you must tell me how Geraldine is getting on. I'll have to go soon to catch the bus and train back to Brighton, but I really don't want to leave you. When I get back I'll have to face Dad's new woman. She's an appalling creature. We call her lots of names behind her back.'

Beryl smiled, and it was such a lovely smile. At that moment, we knew how much we would miss each other.

'I'll never forget what you've done for me,' Beryl whispered, as her eyes welled up again and tears ran down her face. 'I can't thank you enough. I want to give you something before you leave.'

What Beryl did next I have never forgotten. She took her wedding ring from her finger and, holding my hand, pressed the gold band into my palm. She closed my hand around it.

'I want you to have this. Please, Peter.'

I couldn't believe what she had done. I was totally stunned. 'But that's your wedding ring! I can't possibly take that. It should mean something so special to you.'

'I understand what you're saying, but if you don't take it, he'll only go off and sell it for his beer and gambling. I want you to take it, and I know you'll look after it for me.'

'I hope by the time I get to New Zealand you'll have written to me… at least to let me know that you and Geraldine are safe in Brighton with Dad. Please write to me and I'll send it back to you.'

Still, I held the ring tightly in my hand.

I knew I had to leave soon to catch the bus and train. I turned to leave and go down the narrow stairs. We cuddled each other tightly in the doorway, and tears flooded down our cheeks. I didn't want to let go of her. Ever.

Instinctively, I knew Beryl and Geraldine were in real danger in that dreadful, poisonous atmosphere.

What happened at 10 Rillington Place would change my life forever.

Chapter 8
Danger in Rillington Place

I trudged off towards the bus stop, clutching Beryl's wedding ring. I didn't want to take any chances by putting the ring in a pocket or anywhere I couldn't keep a good hold of it. For the whole bus journey, and then on the train from Victoria to Brighton, I held the ring tightly in my clenched fist. This, to me, was a priceless possession, and meant everything. It belonged to Beryl and was so special, even though it carried an indelible link with her cruel husband.

On the way home, I reflected on all the troubles Beryl had told me about. My beloved sister. My head was full of images of how her evil little monster of a husband was treating her. I tried to concentrate on my own treasured memories of Beryl and our childhood.

As the eldest in our family Beryl was petite, pretty and highly intelligent. She had always been a bit on the shy side when it came to men. Beryl would rather meet up with some female pals and go to the cinema. She enjoyed socialising with her friends, but was always more comfortable at home with her family around her. She loved being with us.

Beryl attended Lancaster Road School along with her best friend Joan Vincent, who looked a lot like my sister. They even wore the same type of clothes, and they often swapped items like skirts and blouses. Clothes were rationed in 1941 during the war, and the regulations stayed in place until 1949, so it was common for people to swap items, as they couldn't always buy new outfits. For Beryl and Joan, it was a way to make it look as if they had a lot more clothes than during their teens.

I would often see Beryl wearing something that belonged to Joan, and the other way round. It was quite funny really to witness, and it worked for them, as both girls were petite. Sometimes a friend would say he saw Beryl going along the street with her baby, and it turned out to be Joan, who also had a young child. The same happened when someone thought they saw Joan at the shops, but it was really Beryl wearing some of Joan's clothes.

My sister was always keen on a career that involved short-hand and typing. With the Second World War drawing to a close in the mid-1940s, Beryl had spotted an advert for a telephonist with shorthand and typing skills at Grosvenor House Hotel in Park Lane, Mayfair. It was the perfect opportunity.

Several other young women were after the job, but Beryl impressed at her interview and was offered the position. She knew that many celebrities often stayed there, and she looked forward to meeting them. One of the people she met and spoke to was the Austrian tenor and film actor Richard Tauber. He was the son of a Jewish actor and was proud to perform wherever he could during air raids.

Beryl soon became friends with another telephonist at the Grosvenor House Hotel called Lucy Endicott. Knowing that Beryl was single, and acting entirely in good faith, Lucy set up a blind date for her and one of her friends. What happened next was to change Beryl's life: she went along, and the blind date turned out to be a man called Timothy Evans.

Of all the people in the world she could encounter, it happened to be Timothy Evans who Beryl was set up with. There were educated and elegant people staying at the hotel, who admired and respected Beryl – and yet she was a shy young woman, and Evans won her heart.

Looking for a husband was hard at that time. Men, and good men in particular, were in short supply because of the huge losses during the war. Before the hostilities, she would have had her choice of a wide range of handsome, intelligent suitors. But with thousands from London killed during the fighting, choices after 1945 were very limited indeed. Beryl was only 17 when they met. Evans, on the other hand, was five years older. He was illiterate, with a low IQ. This was not due to any mental health issues, but the result of his lack of education, caused by that foot problem that forced him to spend long periods of his early life in hospital.

As a child, Evans had been swimming in the River Taff in Merthyr Vale, his home village about five miles from the main town of Merthyr Tydfil, when he stepped on glass fragments. At that time, there was no NHS and no way of meeting doctors' fees, so the only option was home treatment. Unfortunately, the hygiene standards were not up to hospital levels, and the wound became infected. Evans soon developed a tubercular verruca on his left foot, causing extensive problems that forced him to miss long periods of his schooling at a time.

Beryl started going out with Evans on a regular basis. My siblings and I were happy for her as long as she was happy, though we noticed that Evans wasn't the sharpest tool in the box. Behind his back, we joked that he was 'a sandwich short of a picnic', and certainly not up to Beryl's level of intelligence. Personally, I found he gave me the creeps, though Basil was happy to go to the pub with him. And most importantly, of course, Beryl seemed to be happy enough in his company.

Evans worked locally as a van driver and delivery man for Lancaster Foods. His family lived in St Mark's Road, only three turnings away from Cambridge Gardens, where we were all living at the time. Evans's side of the family were supportive, and soon grew fond of Beryl. My sister, meanwhile, continued to enjoy her job, contributing towards the housekeeping, keeping in mind, of course, that everything was still on ration.

On 20 September 1947, one day after my big sister's 18th birthday, Beryl and Evans were married at Kensington Register Office. My mother had died six months earlier in March 1947, and never got to see her eldest daughter married. The only people to attend the wedding were Evans's mother, her new partner Penry Probert, his two sisters, my brother Basil, my sister Pat, my father William and me. The witnesses were his sister Eileen and my father.

Beryl looked stunning, as usual, in a light-coloured dress with her dark brown hair in the pageboy style that was popular at the time. Her fantastic smile shone all day.

There were no cars or photographers: it was not a showy affair. We all walked the short distance from the register office to Evans's family home, where the reception took place. Mrs Probert provided a selection of sandwiches and cakes. She put on a good spread, considering that rationing was still in force at the time.

After their wedding, Beryl and Evans lived quite happily with his family in St Mark's Road for a few months. Soon they had some news that would change everything.

'I'm pregnant!' Beryl announced, full of glee. 'Tim and I are going to have a baby. Boy or girl, I don't care. I'm just so excited!'

Everyone was thrilled. Evans and Beryl were delighted, with even my father – not much of a family man – looking forward to the birth of his first grandchild. The only problem was, how could everyone be accommodated in a small house in St Mark's Road?

'We've loved having you here, but you need to find a place of your own,' Mrs Probert said politely but firmly to her son and daughter-in-law. The message was clear enough.

They agreed that it made perfect sense: with a child on the way, they needed to move out and have their own space.

Shortly afterwards, Evans's sister Eileen, on her way home one evening on the train, spotted a 'to let' sign in the window of a top-floor flat, just before she got off the train at Ladbroke-Grove. She could see that the flat was nicely placed between both families at Cambridge Gardens and St Mark's Road. The flat was in a three-storey building, in a cul-de-sac called Rillington Place.

'This is a real step forward,' Beryl told her family and friends excitedly. 'We're going to see a flat. Just imagine our first home together. It will be great for the baby, too.'

Evans and Beryl wasted no time in going to view the flat. Beryl was in the early stages of pregnancy (not, as portrayed at the start of the 1971 film *10 Rillington Place*, carrying a year-old baby). No. 10 was the house at the far end on the left-hand side of the cul-de-sac. It wasn't the most salubrious area, run down after all the bombing, but large areas of London were still to recover.

It was early 1948, only a short time after the war. Times were hard, and nobody had been able to spend the previous years sprucing up their properties. It hadn't crossed many people's minds. Up until 1945, Londoners had simply thought themselves lucky to come out of an air-raid shelter alive and to find they still had a roof over their heads. Many poor souls hadn't been so lucky.

Evans and Beryl knocked at that shabby dark green front door. After a few moments, it was opened, cautiously, by a tall, slim gentleman.

His name was John Reginald Halliday Christie.

'How may I help you?' he asked in that soft voice of his, almost a whisper.

'We've come to view the flat.'

He invited the couple in and introduced himself to them. 'I'm Mr Christie, and this is my wife, Mrs Christie.'

Mrs Christie was a pleasant, middle-aged lady. Her name was Ethel, though initial introductions were more formal.

Mr Christie led the way up the stairs to the second floor.

'There is another tenant, a Mr Kitchener. He's in the flat on the first floor, but he's not a well man and he's often in hospital because of his eyesight. I don't own the building. I act for the landlord, so I can show you what's what.'

He showed Evans and Beryl the flat upstairs. He explained that they had the use of the toilet and wash house on the ground floor outside. Those facilities were accessed by a narrow passage leading past the Christies' kitchen. There was no bath, so it would have to be the wartime tin version.

'Look, the flat is a bit small and it's not what we're looking for,' Evans blurted out. 'We're used to much grander places. I've got good prospects, you know, and I earn decent money. Isn't that right, Beryl?'

Beryl felt embarrassed by his exaggerations, especially when Evans told Christie that his father was an Italian count. She changed the subject and asked if, when she had the baby, she could have use of the garden.

'No, that would infringe regulations in respect of the lease. There is a right of way, so that's not possible.'

This put a dampener on the whole idea of moving into 10 Rillington Place. Christie, sensing this, said another couple were interested in the flat and would be coming round for a look later.

With her baby on the way, Beryl had some misgivings about whether this was truly the right place for them to settle down and start their family. Christie had been very firm about them not using the garden, and she wanted to be able to take the baby outside. Beryl was rather put off, and she felt inclined to look for somewhere else.

However, a decision had to be made quickly. She mulled things over for a few minutes while Evans rattled on. Christie seemed pleasant enough, although that peculiar whispery voice created a strange atmosphere in the room.

'Oh well, we may as well take it,' Evans announced. 'It'll do until we can find something better.'

On the way home, they were excited at the prospect of having their own place to live. When the baby arrived, they would be a proper little family unit. They couldn't wait to break the news; they were full of it.

'I'll help you to clean up and decorate,' Evans's sister Eileen offered when they returned home. 'The three of us should make short work of it.'

Tim and Beryl moved in at Easter time on 28 March 1948. There wasn't too much decorating work to be done. So often, sadly, Timothy and Beryl's flat has been described as 'squalid', but that was not the case at all. The area was run down, but the inside of the flat was in reasonable condition. Pat, Dad and I were now living in Brighton with my father's new woman. However, I knew from my regular trips to see Beryl and Geraldine that their living conditions were nice enough.

Money, though, was tight. Evans earned a reasonable amount for the time; the problem was that he rarely stayed at home to economise. He wasted most of his cash on drinking and putting money on horses or football matches. Beryl had had to give up her job; with the baby on the way, she couldn't add to the household kitty by doing any work.

Over the next few months, as they prepared for the new arrival, Mrs Probert and Evans's sisters helped all they could, and on 10 October 1948, my niece Geraldine was born at Queen Charlotte's Hospital in Goldhawk Road.

As Evans's family were Catholic, it was decided by default that Geraldine would grow up a Catholic, with a traditional baptism. No consideration was shown for the fact that Beryl, like her mother, was of the Jewish faith. The Evans family were fully aware of this, but it was not even discussed.

I had always spent so much time with Beryl when she was still living with us at our home in Cambridge Gardens. We were very close right up until her marriage. But now that she had her own separate family, I began to feel left out and quite lonely. Strangely, I found that I was the only one who ever visited Beryl and Geraldine. Why did my father and my siblings Basil and Pat stay away from Rillington Place? No one else seemed to be looking out for her at a time of such enormous change in her life.

It was around this time that Beryl began to realise just how much Evans was drinking. He had become a regular visitor to the local public houses, and was staying out until late at night, while she was left alone with the baby. Along with the drink came lies, stories and those well-established gambling habits of his.

Poor Beryl was only a teenager, still very naïve, when she first met Evans. He had been her first real boyfriend, and she certainly wasn't worldly or at all streetwise.

It was well known by Evans's own family that he had a violent temper. Even as a child, he had caused difficulties for his parents with his uncontrollable tantrums. These could be attributed to frustration, immaturity and low intelligence.

Beryl, on the other hand, hadn't had the opportunity to gain many household and domestic skills, principally because of the war years. She did her best, cooking, keeping the house in order, and tending to Geraldine's every need.

But all the while, she knew that her husband's extravagant habits were spiralling out of control and rapidly getting them into severe debt. It must have added to the strain to know that her family were no longer just around the corner in Cambridge Gardens. I was unable to pop round and see her whenever I pleased, as I had when they lived on St Mark's Road.

By that November of 1949, I was worrying constantly about Beryl, Geraldine and my impending journey to New Zealand. I thought about boarding the ship and then somehow getting off again before it set sail.

My train pulled into Brighton and, still clutching Beryl's wedding ring, I stepped out onto the platform. I knew that Beryl's situation was dire and that she needed my family's help.

I found Dad as soon as I arrived home.

'I'm desperately worried for Beryl and Geraldine's safety,' I told him. 'Tim is seriously hurting Beryl, and she's very frightened of him. They're in debt because of his drinking and gambling, and he's blaming her!'

Dad listened intently. He said he would pay them a visit, but there was little enthusiasm or genuine concern in his voice. Despite my pleas, I wasn't sure whether he would do anything at all.

On Friday, 4 November 1949, the day before the ship to New Zealand left, Dad accompanied me to The Russell Hotel in Russell Square, where we spent a quiet and uneventful night. I didn't sleep much. My thoughts were bouncing between Beryl and what sort of life lay ahead of me. We had at least managed to discuss the worrying situation facing Beryl and the baby, and I had again encouraged Dad to do something about it, but I still didn't know for certain that he would.

Saturday morning arrived, 5 November. We had an early breakfast, then set off on the bus to Tilbury Docks.

I stood there with my suitcase on the dockside. My father gave me a hug and said, 'Goodbye son', then walked away. There was little or no emotion in his voice. It was as if he was dropping me at school on an ordinary day.

There were about 40 children, and they all had their parents with them. I felt that I had been deserted. When the other children boarded the ship, their parents went with them and had a look round the cabins. But nobody came on board with me. I was on my own. I really felt as if I wasn't wanted.

There was no need for him to go away so quickly. We weren't waiting in the docks for long before boarding. I gritted my teeth, prepared for the voyage, and wished I was in Notting Hill, supporting my sister in the nightmare surroundings of Rillington Place.

After leaving me at Tilbury, Dad went to see Beryl in the evening. It was about teatime. He bumped into Joan Vincent on his way into Rillington Place and they spoke briefly; she had been to visit Beryl with her own baby, and was just leaving. They always took the children out in their prams for a walk together in the park in St Mark's Road.

On this occasion, Beryl and Joan had done another of their clothes swaps: Joan had been to pick up a skirt from Beryl, and while she was there, Beryl broke some news to her.

Another baby was on the way.

Dad and Beryl presumably discussed the impending arrival of her second child. Beryl hadn't talked about the new pregnancy with me, probably because I was so young; she knew I was worried about her and may have thought it would have been too much to take in.

Dad must have been satisfied with Beryl's situation as it was, because he left without concern. He didn't suggest that she should move out of the place, and he didn't seem to think anything was wrong. He disregarded all I had told him and took his visit as confirmation that all was well at Rillington Place.

But by Sunday, 6 November, the severity of the rows had escalated even more. Beryl's life had taken on horrendous new dimensions. With the debts getting out of hand and another baby on the horizon, the atmosphere was becoming intolerable.

Panicking about the prospect of another baby – two mouths to feed, little money to cover the costs, and the constant threat of violence from her husband – Beryl, foolishly, had been trying to terminate her pregnancy with dangerous self-induced methods to procure a miscarriage. She wanted to try to pay for an abortion, but aside from it being illegal at the time, she simply couldn't afford it.

Friends and neighbours noticed how ill she looked, suspected what she had been doing, and tried to dissuade her from making any further attempts. Among those concerned were Reg and Ethel Christie, who took Beryl aside to ask after her wellbeing.

Much has been written about this period of Beryl's life, and some have alleged that Reg Christie spoke to Evans or Beryl, offering to perform an abortion for them. Having had access to crucial documents and scrutinised all the evidence, I feel that to my mind this appears highly unlikely. No one could possibly have witnessed any such conversation.

The only person who might have offered Beryl some support, apart from our father, was her brother Basil, who had stayed in London when Dad, Pat and I moved to Brighton, and still lived nearby. But, sadly, he neglected to check on her and give her the help she so desperately needed. No one was there for Beryl.

In any case, Timothy Evans, as a Roman Catholic, was opposed to abortions and couldn't understand Beryl's despera-tion. Despite his expensive and dangerous habits, he reckoned they could manage with another baby. Perhaps if he had got his priorities in order, and foregone his own personal extravagances, they could have afforded a brother or sister for Geraldine.

That Sunday, Ethel Christie heard a particularly ferocious and violent row upstairs, that lasted on and off through the course of the entire day. Evans did what he did best: he washed and changed, then went to the pub, returning around half past two in the afternoon.

He had some food and went out a couple of hours later to go to the Royalty cinema. It can only be presumed that he saw a film on his own. He returned home around 10 o'clock and went straight to bed.

Many were the times he forced Beryl to have sex with him without consent, usually after he had been drinking. It pained her to tell me this. Marital rape, a truly brutal form of domestic violence, was par for the course in the Evans household.

On the following day, Monday, 7 November, Evans got up at 6am, ready to go to work. Beryl got up shortly afterwards to feed baby Geraldine. Beryl told Evans in no uncertain terms that she had had enough. She was packing her bags and heading to Brighton to stay with her father.

A heated argument broke out, and Evans asked what she was going to do with baby Geraldine.

Beryl, surprised by such a strange question, said that naturally the baby would be going with her to Brighton. 'I can't take any more of your bullying,' she said firmly.

During the course of the day Beryl spoke to Ethel Christie, who saw how terribly ill she was looking and took her in for a chat. Beryl was having trouble with her friend Joan Vincent, Joan had said something untoward, and it had caused Beryl further problems with Evans. As a result, my sister didn't want to see her for a little while.

Most importantly, though, Beryl repeated to Ethel just how unhappy she was, and that she was hoping, somehow, to get out of Rillington Place, especially with a new baby on the way.

Beryl was desperate to get away from Timothy Evans. The day she gave me her wedding ring, really, was proof enough.

Could she ever escape from her violent, controlling husband?

Chapter 9
Murder in 10 Rillington Place

Beryl endured a cold, wet and disappointing day on that Monday, 7 November. There were no workmen around because it had been raining, so they were sent off to carry out interior work elsewhere. The front door of No. 10 was closed, for a change.

Beryl's hopes of making it to the safety of Brighton, and her father's home, had been dashed. She had counted out her cash: it was not enough even for the bus and rail fares.

She and Geraldine would just have to face Evans's vitriol once again.

Beryl wondered if she could have managed the journey, even with enough money. She was feeling tired, unwell and anxious. Her main anxiety stemmed from the fact that Evans would soon be home from work. Her entire body would have been shaking with fear and trepidation.

I saw with my own eyes how frightened she had been the Wednesday before. Today, she was even worse.

I firmly believe that, at about 5.30pm, Beryl was in the kitchen, preparing Geraldine's tea, when she heard her husband coming up the stairs. He would have gone straight into the bedroom to see Geraldine. As usual, my lovely niece bounced up and down in the cot, full of excitement. At around this time, the Christies left the house and went off to the cinema.

'What are you doing here?' Evans no doubt snapped when he saw her. 'Thought you were going to Brighton, weren't you?'

'And you would be here, doing as you like?' Beryl would have replied, knowing my feisty sister.

His usual tactic was to turn round and give her a slap across the face – the normal greeting when he arrived home from work.

What I am about to tell you is shocking. Of course, only my sister and Evans were involved in this particular fracas; from what she told me, my version of events all adds up. Remember that I had information from Beryl, my brother Basil and crucial documents from the time. I've also been able to piece together damning comments from neighbours who knew all about my violent brother-in-law.

Even the officer in charge of the case later declared that, taking all the evidence into account, no one was involved in carrying out an abortion for my sister. And so much has been written about a fictitious abortion. I can confirm that this is all backed up by pathology reports from the period.

In one of his many police statements Evans even admits strangling Beryl with a piece of rope and her baby with a tie. This is probably one of the few times that he told the truth.

So I am quite confident in saying that Evans went through to the kitchen, prepared some supper for himself, got changed and headed out to the Kensington Park Hotel, known locally as the KPH.

Beryl heard the Christies come back in at about 9.30pm, but Evans stayed out at the pub until closing time an hour later. He'd been drinking, bragging and romanticising to the amusement of many that evening.

Over the course of the day the debts, Beryl's proposed Brighton trip, and everything else going wrong in his life had played on his mind. When the pub closed, Evans made his way back home, 'well oiled' by now. Beryl was pottering around, just about to get ready for bed, when he appeared in the doorway.

I am convinced that, as soon as he was indoors, it all kicked off – about anything and everything. She couldn't say or do anything right. He kept slapping her in the face and body as he shouted at her. She became desperately frightened as he screamed at her.

My belief is that Evans grabbed her round the neck and she struggled to get free, but he overpowered her.

He was fuelled with drink and totally out of control. She managed momentarily to break free, but it was no good. There was nowhere to go, she was trapped, and he wasn't letting up. I believe Evans punched her twice in the face with the full force of his fist, causing severe injuries to her eye, nose and mouth. Beryl collapsed to the floor, with blood pouring from her wounds, her face swelling into bruises. She wasn't moving.

Evans made no attempt to check she was all right. He failed to help her, not realising just how much damage he had caused. Those injures are all backed up by the pathology reports and, sadly, horrific pictures from the mortuary.

I hope and pray that little Geraldine stayed asleep through all of this. The kitchen became a battleground. Beryl had taken the full brunt of the force, but somehow she still managed to get back to her feet.

How long she had been unconscious, we will never know. In agonising pain and utterly dazed, she didn't realise he was standing behind her.

Evans made a further grab for my sister, picking up a piece of rope and forcing it round her throat. He pulled it tighter and tighter.

Beryl was beyond fighting him off. She had no fight left in her. As he continued to tighten the rope, he must have watched as life finally ebbed from her young body.

It was over.

The Christies would have heard the commotion from their flat downstairs. The rest of the neighbours later remarked on the awful racket that took place that particular night. Rows were commonplace, but this was something different.

Timothy Evans was yet to realise the awful magnitude of what he had done. What would he do when the drink wore off, and he was faced with the horrendous reality that he had killed his wife? What if the Christies had woken up? They had surely heard the row.

Evans was faced with a dilemma. What was he going to do with Beryl's body? In a house so small, it wasn't going to be long before the Christies found out. What about Geraldine, poor little soul? What fate lay in store for the helpless little cherub?

Evans had his work cut out. His system was still awash with drink, but the gravity of his actions were beginning to dawn on him. Sleep was out of the question, and he was now faced with looking after little Geraldine all alone. How could he prevent her from crying, and drawing attention to the absence of her devoted mother?

He would have remembered that Mr Kitchener, the tenant who occupied the first-floor flat, was in hospital. Mr Kitchener usually left his kitchen door unlocked, as people did at the time, without fear of being burgled.

Evans decided, with little thought as always, to move Beryl's body down into Mr Kitchener's kitchen. The question was, how? It would be an extremely difficult task on his own – he was a small man and could not carry her alone.

The staircase was narrow and steep. His only option was to drag her down the stairs, walking backwards. With his small stature, it was quite precarious. But he decided that there was nothing else for it.

Her feet banged down every stair, as he dragged her down to the first floor and across the short landing into the kitchen.

On the ground floor, the Christies were awakened by a 'loud thumping noise' in the middle of the night: it was 'as if someone was moving heavy furniture about'. They resigned themselves to the fact that that couldn't be the case: Ethel Christie wondered if the couple might be doing a 'moonlight flit', given their financial difficulties. Reg Christie got up and looked out of the window, but he couldn't see anyone coming or going, and the noise eventually stopped. Reg and Ethel went back to sleep.

Evans left Beryl's body there, shut the door and went back upstairs. He hadn't slept, and it wouldn't be too long before he had to get ready for work.

But what about Geraldine? he suddenly thought. He would have to feed and change her and get her dressed before he left in his van. Could he leave her on her own? Where would he say Beryl was? So many decisions to make, and so little time. He made himself a cup of tea, as he always did, and contemplated his next move.

He realised he would either have to go to work or find some excuse not to turn up. For Evans, that wouldn't have been too difficult: he was full of bogus stories, lies and excuses. The biggest problem was going to be explaining the whereabouts of Beryl. More to the point, what was he going to do with her body? He couldn't leave her in Mr Kitchener's flat for long; Mr Kitchener might return from hospital any day. What would he tell the Christies? All these questions churned over in his mind, and he needed to find some answers.

Evans was up most mornings at about 6am. Beryl was usually up soon afterwards, ready to feed Geraldine and prepare for the day ahead.

His day had to look much the same, so as not to arouse suspicion. He washed, changed and decided that he would go into work as usual and drive around in his delivery van. He dressed and fed Geraldine, then left her tucked in her cot. On this occasion he locked the kitchen door behind him, which was unusual, and went downstairs as normal on his way to work.

The workmen were back at around 8.30am that day, Tuesday, 8 November 1949, to continue the jobs on the wash house. Beryl's friend Joan Vincent called in to Rillington Place around lunchtime to see her. She was upset about their disagreement, and wanted to put it right and make amends. Joan was a kind young woman, and whatever it was that she had said to upset Beryl, it wouldn't have been meant with malice. I know the background from her statements.

The front door was open for the builders' access, so Joan went straight upstairs to Beryl's flat. She found the kitchen door shut. She had a feeling that someone was inside, holding the handle. It did not occur to her that the door might be locked;

it was never locked. Joan was used to walking straight into the kitchen most days, and this stubborn door worried her. The bedroom door was shut, and she didn't want to intrude. If she had gone in, she would have discovered Geraldine asleep.

'Are you there, Beryl?' she asked tentatively.

No answer.

'Beryl, I'm so sorry about our falling out. Let's make up. Please.'

Still no answer.

'I am sure somebody is in there, and if you don't want to open the door, you needn't.'

Joan could see Ethel hovering downstairs. Ethel was used to seeing Joan coming and going, and normally thought nothing of it, because the young women were such good friends. Joan, like me, would often chat to Ethel or Reg downstairs in the passage if she was waiting for my sister to come home. But on this occasion Ethel had heard Joan talking outside the door, and was concerned to find out what was going on.

'Someone is in the kitchen holding the door shut,' Joan told Ethel. 'Is it Beryl, do you think? It must be Beryl. We had a slight falling out, but I thought we could make it up.'

'It can only be Beryl at this time of day,' Ethel said, thoughtfully. 'Tim will be at work. I haven't seen her go out, so she must be in there. I'm sure she just needs some space.'

Throughout that Tuesday, no one saw Beryl, not even the Christies. Ethel heard Geraldine crying on and off, but assumed that was what babies did, so she decided not to interfere. Ethel was genuinely worried that she hadn't seen Beryl. She also knew that, because of the pregnancy and many attempts to abort the baby herself, my sister had been looking really ill. I have no doubt that she would have expressed those concerns to her husband.

At about 5.30pm, I believe Evans came home from work and found Christie waiting to speak to him. He asked about all the banging in the early hours. It had disturbed Christie and his wife.

'The neighbours are making complaints all the time,' Christie said in his normal hushed tone. 'If things continue like this then you, Beryl and the baby will have to move on.'

Christie must have asked Evans about Beryl's welfare, as she hadn't been seen all day. He mentioned that Ethel thought Beryl looked ill the last time she saw her. Geraldine had also been crying a lot, and that would have concerned the Christies.

Evans would have offered his standard response. 'Sorry about last night, Mr Christie. I had been out for a drink in the evening. I got back about half past ten and as soon as I got in Beryl started a row about the money.'

Beryl had told me before that this was the normal pattern of conversation: Evans always found a way to turn the blame on her. The day in question was no different. Except for the fact that my loving, caring, beautiful sister had been murdered.

So where had Beryl been all day? Christie must have wondered. Evans, I am certain, would have said she was out with friends, leaving Geraldine on her own – something that he claimed happened regularly, though that was not true.

'That girl!' Evans continued. 'I'll have a word with her, Mr Christie.'

Timothy Evans was predictable in conversation. Reg was persistent, and pressed him for more details about the banging in the night.

Reality flooded back as Evans reflected on the events of the evening before. How could he lie his way out of this one? He was faced with a dilemma, and it must have shown in his face.

'It was like this, Mr Christie: we had this terrible row and I slapped her in the face with my hand and she picked up a bottle to throw at me. I grabbed it from her.'

He would have confessed to punching her full in the face with his fist, causing those severe injuries to her eye, nose and mouth.

He couldn't resist the truth any longer. Evans, I have no doubt, told Reg Christie how he had strangled his wife with a rope.

Christie, realising at once the gravity of what Evans was telling him, would have wasted no time in hurrying up to Mr Kitchener's flat, with Evans limping along behind. Opening the kitchen door, they saw Beryl's lifeless body lying on the floor, uncovered. The severe injuries to her face were evident, and there were gruesome marks around her neck where she had been strangled.

Seeing this, Christie must have died a thousand deaths. He knew that he could not report Evans to the police. Evans could never have known, but Reg Christie was hiding dark secrets of his own in 10 Rillington Place.

Christie could not risk having the police crawling all over the house. At that moment, he knew he had no choice but to assist Evans, whatever that might entail, to conceal this horrendous crime.

Christie must have hidden Beryl's body with a small cover he found in Mr Kitchener's flat. He told Evans that the body couldn't stay in there, because the tenant might return from hospital at any time.

Neither of them knew how they could dispose of the body, especially as the builders were still scheduled to work for a few more days. Nothing could be done to raise any suspicion. They closed the door and went up to Evans's flat, where they would have had a cup of tea while discussing what to do next. Evans, a cruel and callous father, finally fed and changed Geraldine, who by now was distressed from having spent such a long time alone in her cot.

Evans showed no real signs of remorse for what he had done. He had threatened to kill Beryl on a number of occasions, and now he had gone through with it. Christie must have impressed on him the serious consequences of committing murder; by now, he knew that he was also implicated as an accessory.

Later on Tuesday evening, once Geraldine was asleep, Evans returned to old habits. He got changed and went to the pub for his daily drink.

Reg Christie told Ethel the sordid details of what had happened. Clearly distressed by it all, they would have sat talking about the fact that Evans's continual violence had led to the tragedy. He persuaded her that having the police around was not a good idea.

Naturally, Ethel was upset at the thought of Beryl's body being left as it was. After all, they were both very fond of her and Geraldine. So Christie went upstairs and found a thick blanket in Mr Kitchener's flat, which he proceeded to wrap Beryl up in.

Christie used cord to secure the covering with noticeable swiftness; he had worked for the Post Office and knew how to wrap parcels securely. Bizarrely, he carried out this task with a certain dignity. Christie, knowing how gullible Evans was, may have suggested 'putting the body down the manhole' at the front of the house, but there is no way of knowing this for certain.

The following morning, Wednesday, 9 November, Evans got up and made a cup of tea and had a smoke as usual. He changed and fed Geraldine, made some breakfast for himself, and then headed out to work in his delivery van. All day Geraldine was left alone, unchanged and unfed, and crying. At about 6.30pm, he came home as usual, fed and changed Geraldine, and went out for a drink again. I do wonder how much he really fed her, because shopping wasn't one of his regular activities.

Wednesday evenings had been the one opportunity in the week that Evans and Beryl occasionally took to go to the cinema.

It was a rare opportunity for Beryl to escape all the trauma trapping her at home. On the way, they would take Geraldine to Mrs Probert, Evans's mother. If Mrs Probert was busy, Ethel Christie babysat Geraldine instead. My brother Basil worked as a projectionist at the Royalty cinema, and Beryl and Evans had recently seen Graham Greene's spy thriller The Third Man. Beryl had wanted to see the American blockbuster Samson and Delilah, but that wasn't due to be shown until 1950. She never got to see it.

Mrs Probert always enjoyed spending a few hours with my niece before Evans and Beryl collected her on the way home from the cinema. On that Wednesday evening, 9 November, Mrs Probert was surprised when Evans called round to see her on his own after his usual pub visit.

'Beryl and Geraldine have gone to Brighton for a holiday,' he slurred. 'They're staying with Beryl's dad. I don't think they'll be back for a week or two.'

Mrs Probert said she felt hurt, not having seen her daughter-in-law and granddaughter before they left. This holiday was most unusual, especially as it had come without warning.

'I do apologise, Mam. Look, there wasn't time for them to see you. Beryl will write, though. I'll make sure of that.'

Mrs Probert accepted what he said. However, she knew only too well that Evans had managed to get away with lie after lie all his life. Was this another of his deceptions?

She gave him the benefit of the doubt. Why would he lie about something like that? Her daughters convinced her that Beryl and Geraldine must have gone to Brighton, as Evans said.

Evans seemed able to carry on as if nothing had happened. He continued with his normal routine, getting up and going to work each day. I often wonder how well he attended to the baby. How awful it must have been for Geraldine to be left alone like that, with nobody to look after her. People who heard her crying just assumed that Beryl was there, doing her best to appease the little one.

There is one detail I still cannot be sure of: did Geraldine witness any part of the brutal attack on her mother, or was she asleep? There is no way of knowing. I can only hope she could not see what was happening in the kitchen.

But I do know for certain: Geraldine's own life was now in danger inside 10 Rillington Place.

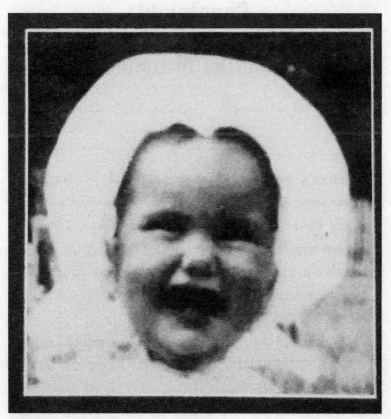

Geraldine pictured shortly before her death.

Chapter 10
The Murder of Geraldine

Geraldine, poor little soul, had become fretful and was crying inconsolably. And a young child doesn't cry incessantly for no reason. It was only a matter of time before the neighbours decided to do something about the baby's plight. Reg Christie had already told Evans that he couldn't leave her alone for so long. All Evans was capable of saying was: 'What can I do, Mr Christie?'

Christie told him that he needed do something; he needed to have her looked after. Evans was a totally incompetent father, and now boxed into a corner. He couldn't ask his mother or sisters because of the lies he had already told them about Beryl going on holiday to Brighton with Geraldine.

After Evans left his mother's house on Wednesday evening, he couldn't resist the temptation of a few extra drinks in the KPH. Stress and frustration were by now eating away at him.

He had no idea of how to cope with the situation. Geraldine was becoming an encumbrance. His feeding and caring had become erratic. She needed cuddles and someone to play with. She required proper attention, like any baby. And yet she had nothing, not even her mummy.

Neighbours continued to question where Beryl was. 'What's wrong with Geraldine? Where's Beryl? Is she looking after the baby?'

The lies kept coming, he began to tell conflicting stories, and suspicion continued to grow.

When he approached 10 Rillington Place late on that Wednesday evening, he would have heard his child's cries. So would everybody in the street.

As he got nearer, the cries became louder. The sound of her incessant screaming, combined with the drink, heightened Evans's vile temper. He was full of confidence once more. He let himself in the door and went straight upstairs, where Geraldine was breaking her little heart.

Hearing footsteps, she stopped crying and became excited. Her daddy was home, he would feed her, they would have hugs and cuddles and play together. She was a happy little bird now, in an ideal world, about to see her father.

But her father no longer wanted her. Evans crashed through the door and grabbed the sweet, once happy little angel from her cot.

He took his tie, tied it tightly around her tender little neck, and silenced her for the last time.

Evans left Geraldine's lifeless body in her cot. Once again, with alcohol swilling round in his system, he had to think clearly and quickly about how to disguise another hideous crime. His wife and daughter were dead, and he had to contemplate his next move very carefully. Evans took Geraldine's precious little body downstairs to Mr Kitchener's flat and laid his daughter beside Beryl. We will never know what was going through his head as he closed Mr Kitchener's door.

On Thursday, 10 November, Evans went to work as usual, with his daughter no longer there to plague his conscience with her cries. With both of them lying in Mr Kitchener's flat, Evans could please himself.

Evans was still in dire need of money to fund his excessive drinking and gambling habits, which showed no signs of abating. He was still going in and out of bookmakers' shops as well as filling in his football pools coupons.

Beryl usually picked up her husband's wages from his employer, Mr Adler, every Friday evening. She collected them on his behalf because, if he was working extra hours on a Friday, he would return from his rounds too late to be paid.

Now Evans needed his money more than ever, and he wasn't prepared to wait until Friday. And, of course, my sister wouldn't be collecting it for him this time. On his return from his day's work that Thursday, he was determined to make a point of speaking to his boss, Mr Adler. Evans said he wanted his money a day early, claiming that 'he needed to post it somewhere'.

Mr Adler, well aware of Evans's lack of intelligence and tendency to invent stories, asked him how he intended to do that.

Evans replied that he was going to send it by registered post.

Mr Adler said that sending the money by post would be all right, but Evans would be paid his wages in the usual way, to his wife on the Friday.

'If you don't give me my money now, I won't drive for you any more,' Evans shot back.

Mr Adler was more than ready with his answer. Evans's work had been poor recently. He had returned with undelivered orders, leading to complaints from customers. Mr Adler told Evans that his work as a food delivery driver had been most unsatisfactory.

'I don't care,' Evans replied. 'I've got a much better job to go to anyway.'

The boss was brief and to the point. He said the contract was terminated with immediate effect, and handed over all wages due. 'You can come in tomorrow to collect your cards.'

Meanwhile Joan Vincent, still concerned at the lack of contact from Beryl, had returned to Rillington Place on the Thursday. This was most unlike her friend. They had had a tiff, but that could be sorted out, surely? The front door was unlocked, so she went inside and climbed the stairs. This time Reg Christie was waiting on the second-floor landing, probably trying to find out about Geraldine.

'What do you want?' he asked in that whispery voice.

'I've come to see Beryl again,' Joan said. 'Is she not in? Do you know where she is?'

'Beryl has gone to Bristol with Geraldine,' Christie answered quickly. 'I don't know when she'll be back.'

There was something sinister in his voice. Those piercing eyes seemed to be staring right into her. What was he hiding? Despondent, Joan headed back down the stairs, out of the front door and into Rillington Place. Who did Beryl know in Bristol? Her father lived in Brighton – why would she be in Bristol?

Evans, now with a pocketful of cash, was already in the pub. The KPH's best customer needed to drown his sorrows.

In the ground-floor flat at 10 Rillington Place, the Christies realised that they hadn't heard baby Geraldine crying at all. Ethel was concerned because Evans had been out such a lot. The pram, usually kept in the Christies' front room, to save Beryl having to carry it upstairs every time, was still there, untouched. The other neighbours assumed from the lack of crying that Beryl had indeed gone away with Geraldine.

From my experience, the Christies seemed fond of Beryl and Geraldine. They had seen with their own eyes the difficulties she endured, living with a drunk and violent husband. Concerned for the baby's welfare, Ethel went to the bottom of the stairs and listened for Geraldine, as she often did. There was no sound. Instinctively she felt something was wrong, and asked Christie to take a look. He climbed up to Evans's flat. There was no sign of Geraldine; her cot was empty.

He checked inside Mr Kitchener's flat.

The sight before him was horrific. There, alongside the body of Beryl, lay the uncovered body of baby Geraldine with a tie wrapped tightly around her little neck. She, too, had been strangled.

Reg came out, shut the door behind him, and headed downstairs to tell Ethel.

Meanwhile the workmen had been coming and going all day, so the front door was open once more to allow them access. Joan Vincent, back for yet another visit although it was getting dark, went straight upstairs once more.

Christie met her on the first-floor landing this time, and was quite abrupt. Beryl and Geraldine had gone to Bristol, as he had told her before. He more or less hissed at her in that whispery voice of his, and Joan left again. This time, she was more than disturbed by the reception she had received.

Geraldine, my gorgeous little niece, had suffered the same fate as my beautiful sister. They had both been silenced forever by Timothy Evans.

On Friday morning, 11 November, Evans met with my brother Basil in the cafe opposite the Royalty cinema. Basil later described him as 'ashen-faced and agitated'. Evans told him that he was going to Bristol on the following Monday, 14 November, to see Beryl and Geraldine.

Basil must have known that this was a load of nonsense. What could they possibly be doing in Bristol? During their previous meeting only a couple of days before, Evans had told Basil they had gone to Brighton and would be staying with her father for a week or two.

Evans also told Basil that he had gone round to see Beryl's grandmother and aunt, who lived at 13 Bonchurch Road, Ladbroke Grove. Evans had made excuses about his wife not coming over for lunch on Tuesday, 7 November. He told them that they had gone to Scotland for a holiday. The stories kept on coming.

Basil regarded his brother-in-law's demeanour as nervous and contradictory. Feeling uneasy, and sensing something was wrong, Basil's immediate port of call should have been Rillington Place, to satisfy himself that everything was all right. Why my brother failed to do that, I will never know. Basil did contact his father in Brighton, however, asking if Beryl and Geraldine were staying with him. The answer unsettled him even more.

Basil also went round to see Mrs Probert and Evans's sisters at St Mark's Road, expressing his concerns and suggesting that perhaps the police should be contacted. The local police station was less than half a mile away. Why didn't he just go himself? The situation was becoming urgent: no one had seen Beryl or

Geraldine for several days, and their alleged whereabouts were changing all the time.

Evans returned to Rillington Place sometime on Friday, and asked one of the workmen how long it would take to finish their job. He was told 'a couple of days'. He was keen to get a firm answer, making it known that he was leaving Rillington Place the following Monday, 14 November.

He still had to do something about the bodies, and he needed the workers out of the way first. Beryl and Geraldine were still lying in Mr Kitchener's flat, and the poorly tenant might return to Rillington Place at any time.

Evans became desperately eager to see the workers finish. They were still replacing floor joists, floorboards and skirting boards in the hallway downstairs. Some floorboards also needed replacing in Christie's front room. Only then would the workers be gone.

While Evans stood in the passageway, Ethel came out, telling him to be careful. The boards still hadn't all been replaced. She shone a torch to show him where to tread.

There was little conversation between them. After all, what could she say? Reg Christie would not want her to get too involved, but that was becoming extremely difficult. Evans told her that he had packed his job in and planned to leave on the Monday.

Timothy Evans was getting more and more anxious. He would be leaving Rillington Place very soon, and still had two bodies to get rid of. His problem: how and where? He had no van now that he had left his job, so that limited his options. Should he approach Reg Christie and hope he might help him out?

As Evans was about to go upstairs Christie called him, saying he wanted a word. The conversation must have revolved around where to move the two bodies. They resolved to put them in the wash house.

The builders finished the works, clearing and removing their tools from the wash house where they had kept them, early on Saturday, 12 November. Before leaving, one of the workmen offered Christie some old floorboards, which had now been replaced, for firewood.

That Saturday, finally, was the opportunity that Evans needed to move the bodies. Christie had made sure that Beryl's body was already neatly tied up. Still, it would take more than one person, especially given the disabilities Evans and Christie had between them – one with a dodgy foot and the other a dodgy back. Neither one could have carried Beryl's body down to the wash house alone.

The operation meant negotiating the steep, narrow staircase down from the first floor. This entailed a short flight of stairs to a small landing, then a turn to go down the full flight of 14 stairs to the ground-floor passageway, then a tight 90-degree turn into an even narrower passage past Christie's kitchen. Then through the back door to the right, which led out to the wash house and garden area. In all, the distance was about 30 feet from the bottom of the stairs.

There, between them, they put Beryl's body in the small space underneath the sink. They covered her by leaning the bits of floorboards, left behind by the builders for firewood, up against the front of the sink.

For Evans, it was a job almost done; he only had baby Geraldine to take care of. He went upstairs, picked up the body of his daughter and carried her to the wash house. He left Geraldine on the floor behind the door like a bundle of rags, with some fragments of wood on top.

During the day, Christie sought treatment from his local GP, Dr Odess in Coleville Square, as he did several times a week. He complained of severe back pain, known as fibrositis. This could have been a consequence of straining to help Evans to move Beryl's body. In an effort to relieve his discomfort, the doctor 'strapped him up'; perhaps Christie wanted to conceal any injuries sustained in the secret operation on the stairs.

We can safely assume that Evans spent the rest of Saturday feeling pleased with all he had achieved, and decided to treat himself to an evening at the pub. By all accounts, it was no effort for him to consume at least five or six pints at a time. Besides, he had nothing to worry about any more, or so his lack of brain-power told him.

On that same Saturday evening, Evans called round to see his mother. When he arrived, Mrs Probert asked him if he was all right, because he was singing.

He told her that he was happy because of his trip to Brighton on Monday to see Beryl and Geraldine. Then he hesitated. 'I have sent her 30 shillings, so I don't know if I'll have enough left to get to Brighton.'

She asked if he was in any trouble. He said everything was fine, and she gave him enough money for the bus and train fare from London.

Evans called on a Mr Hookway, a furniture dealer at 319 Portobello Road. Evans said he had bought some furniture in Cardiff, but it was no longer needed and he wanted to sell it all. In reality, the furniture had originally come from a shop in Hammersmith, and Evans had not actually bought it, but had it on hire purchase. His mother stood as guarantor for the finance.

It was agreed that Mr Hookway should come round to Rillington Place on the Sunday to collect the furniture. Evans said he wanted £65 for it – a sizeable sum at the time – but Mr Hookway decided it was only worth £40, and that was all he was prepared to pay.

Mr Hookway insisted on seeing the original receipt for the furniture to prove that Evans owned it himself. Evans insisted that he was the rightful owner. He said he was going to Bristol on Monday to a new job, and he would get his wife, who was already down there, to send on the receipt.

The deal was done.

It was arranged that the furniture would be collected on Monday morning. That fitted in well with Evans's plans, although it was not yet clear where he was going. So far, he had told various people that Beryl was in Brighton, Bristol and Scotland.

Just after Mr Hookway had left, a Mr Mackay appeared and Evans told him to come upstairs. He was from the hire purchase company, and had come to collect the latest payment on the furniture. It was unusual to call on a Sunday, but Evans was difficult to pin down at the best of times. Mr Mackay evidently thought he could catch this bad payer unawares. The hire purchase man said he thought that Evans looked 'rather frustrated', but assumed it was down to a heavy drinking session the previous evening.

Evans paid him his money on this occasion, at the same time telling him that his wife and daughter were in Bristol. Of course, he gave no indication that he had sold the furniture, or that the flat would shortly be cleared and vacated.

On Monday, 14 November, Mr Hookway arrived to collect the furniture. He paid Evans the £40 they had agreed, and asked him to sign the receipt, which he did, giving his address as 79 Whiteladies Road, Bristol. There is a Whiteladies Road in Bristol; maybe he looked it up on a map, although he couldn't read very well.

Another caller that day was Albert Rollings, a rag dealer who took away some clothes and sundry rags. He left 'a drink' – a small amount of money to help with the substantial bar bills.

At some time during the day, Evans took his packed suitcase to Paddington Station, where he deposited it in the 'left luggage' department. In the afternoon he went to the Royalty cinema, where Basil still worked, and later that evening they had a meal together.

Evans told him he had received a telegram from Beryl.

'Geraldine is ill,' Evans said to Basil. 'I'll have to go to Bristol. That's where she and Geraldine are staying, so I'll have to go there.'

Basil was confused because of all the different stories. The Bristol story was obviously made up, and there was no telegram to show. As Evans was leaving, Basil caught sight of a cloakroom ticket from Paddington, but never queried the route to be taken.

Bristol was never part of the plan. Evans made his way to the station, where he collected his case and caught the 12.55am train to Merthyr Tydfil, Wales, via Cardiff. He was due to arrive at about 6.30am on the Tuesday morning. Whatever Basil thought, believed or knew up until this point, one thing became clear to him: there was a strong possibility that something bad had happened to Beryl and Geraldine. I am positive that he suspected Timothy Evans was involved in some way.

Merthyr Tydfil was the home of Mrs Probert's brother and sister-in-law, Mr and Mrs Lynch. Merthyr was totally familiar to him, as he was brought up there.

Evans's uncle and aunt were surprised to see him. Apparently, they hadn't seen him for several years. They asked what he was doing down in Wales. He said he was on a trip with his boss, on business, but their car had broken down.

'The big end, I think it is,' he told Mr and Mrs Lynch. 'It's being repaired, though.'

It was only a matter of time before Evans would be caught out with his lies and stories. The family knew he was a compulsive liar from a very early age.

Oddly, he arrived without a suitcase, despite the fact that he was obviously intending to stay in the area, if only on business. Knowing that he would be staying with his uncle and aunt for a few days, he would have at least needed clean clothes.

Shortly after Evans arrived at the Lynch home, his uncle saw he had a cloakroom ticket for a suitcase, which he had deposited at Cardiff railway station. Why had he left his suitcase in Cardiff? I've always wondered what was inside the suitcase. Perhaps it contained items belonging to Beryl or Geraldine.

One morning during breakfast, Evans told his aunt that Beryl and Geraldine were staying with her father in Brighton until after Christmas.

On Thursday, 17 November, he supposedly went to Cardiff for the purpose of finding out 'when the repairs to the car would be finished'. He reappeared later in the day, having bought a new shirt and a jazzy tie.

He showed no signs of being upset. On the contrary, he was in good spirits, visiting the local pubs with his uncle, and even joining in with the singsongs. Some evenings were spent with a cousin, William Costigan, and his wife.

On the Friday, while they were all in a public house in Merthyr Vale, Evans took out of his pocket a gold wedding ring. He asked his uncle if he thought the landlord might give him a bit of cash for it. When questioned, he denied that it was Beryl's ring. He said he had found it in Gloucester. When Mrs Lynch saw the ring, again he denied that it was his wife's prized possession. He said he had found it in either Cheltenham or Gloucester.

The ring, from wherever he acquired it, certainly wasn't Beryl's. I was taking good care of the genuine article. It was later established that Evans sold yet another ring to a Mr Scannell, a jeweller in Merthyr Vale, for six shillings. The jeweller said he had also been offered a watch, but he had decided not to take it.

Back in Rillington Place, Christie was still suffering with his bad back. Dr Odess referred his patient for a hospital appointment. Day after day, he continued to suffer from back pain.

The doctor received a letter from the registrar of St Thomas' Hospital: 'On examination I found he was in agony whenever he tried to bend down or bring the left lumbar muscles into use. This is a case of muscular pain and I was able to give him considerable relief by an injection of local anaesthetic. I have referred him to the physiotherapy department.'

In Wales, Mr and Mrs Lynch were clearly not comfortable with Evans's general demeanour. Mr Lynch suggested to his wife that she should write to his sister in London and find out what was going on. She told her sister-in-law in the letter that Evans had been with them since 15 November. Beryl and Geraldine were not with him, so what was going on?

Apparently, Mrs Probert burned the letter she received, although we don't know why. I think her anger and frustrations over her son's behaviour boiled over. Her reply was accompanied by a short note from Evans's sister Maureen. The note made the family's position perfectly clear:

Mam is going to write to you, Aunty Vi, and she will tell you about Tim. I know if I see him I'll kill him for the worry he's giving Mam.

The envelope also contained a letter from Thomasina Probert to her brother Cornelius Lynch and sister-in-law Vi. It was posted to their address where Evans was staying, Mount Pleasant in Merthyr Vale.

Dear Brother Sister

Just a few lines in answer to your welcome letter which I got safe. Well Vi, I don't know what lies Tim have told you down there. I know nothing about him as I have not seen him for three weeks and I have not seen Beryl or the baby for a month. Tim came round and told me that Beryl and the baby had gone to Brighton to her father for a holiday, that is all I know about them, ask Tim what he have done with the Furnichter he took from his flat, there is some mystery about him, you can tell him from me he don't want to come to me. I never want to see him again as long as I live. He have put years on my life since last August. He knows what I mean, he packed up a good job up here. He is like his father, no good to himself or anybody else. If you are mug enough to keep him for nothing, well that will be your fault. I don't intend to keep him any more. I have done my best for him and Beryl, what thanks did I get? His name stinks up here. Everywhere I go people are asking for money he owes them. I am ashamed to say he is my son. You can also tell him he won't get anything from the Loan Club. I am paying his debts with it. The furniture man have been, so I payed £20 to him. I will send Tim the bill in my next letter. I think I have told you all the news for now. I will close with love from your loving sister.'

Beryl's friend Lucy Endicott later stated that Evans hated his mother 'like poison'. This was partly because she always took Beryl's side in an argument. It was also true that, on several occasions, his mother had been known to give her son a good slap for the way he bullied Beryl.

Sunday, 20 November 1949 was Evans's 25th birthday. Not much is known about that day, but one can only guess that he might have spent it with a glass in his hand.

While Evans was in Merthyr, the arrears on his furniture, which he had already sold for £40, were beginning to mount up. The man who collected the payments tried to contact him, with no success. He turned to Mrs Probert, who had foolishly stood as guarantor, and informed her that the amount owed in total was £48 15s. She was responsible for the arrears, and had to come to some arrangement. I don't know how she paid it off, or how much she could afford.

On Monday, 21 November, Evans left the Lynch household and headed back to London.

Numerous books and articles have speculated about his return trip to London. Some state that he went back to Rillington Place, with stories that he was looking for a job, as he had spent all his money. Why would he have gone back to Rillington Place? After all, the Christies knew what he had done. He was probably the last person they wanted to see.

It is most likely that he met up with my brother Basil and bought a suitcase from him.

It is strange that Basil, having expressed serious concerns previously about the welfare and whereabouts of his sister and niece, continued to do nothing. He had already learned from his father that Beryl and Geraldine were not in Brighton. And yet Basil seemed to be taken in by the lies and deceit, apparently comfortable in Evans's company. It is important to remember that, since 7 November 1949, Timothy Evans, Beryl and Geraldine had not been seen together.

Evans returned to Merthyr on 23 November with his new suitcase, saying that he had visited his mother while in London. He said he had been to see Beryl, but that as he entered, she had walked out without saying a word, leaving the baby in her cot.

Evans told some people that he had taken little Geraldine to stay with a couple from Newport who were living in London, and that he had paid them £15. He claimed that he hadn't taken the baby to his mother because she was working, and that it didn't enter his head to take her with him to his aunt's house.

I believe that the day after Evans returned to Merthyr Tydfil, 24 November, he was in the pub, drinking with his uncle and his cousins the Costigans. Evans presented Mrs Costigan with the gift of a necklace, which looked new and pretty.

He said to her: 'Don't ask no questions where it come from, because I won't tell you.'

The necklace was actually an inexpensive present that Beryl had been given by her mother-in-law, Mrs Probert.

Evans, sporting a new camel-hair coat, costing most of the proceeds from the sale of his furniture, with his hair slicked down, was acting like 'Jack the Lad'. He was handing out lavish presents of jewellery that had once belonged to his murdered wife.

One morning at the breakfast table, Mr and Mrs Lynch said to Evans that they had written to Mr Thorley, my father, in Brighton, and that they had received a telegram, which his aunt read to him.

William said that neither Beryl nor Geraldine were with him in Brighton and that he had not seen them since the summer. It was strange he should say that, having visited her during the early evening on 5 November, 1949. That was the day he took me to Tilbury to board the ship to New Zealand.

Evans, apparently, had one of his usual temper tantrums; he had been put on the spot. Angrily he asked them why they had contacted Beryl's father, saying it was none of their business.

Scrambling for excuses, he announced that Beryl had left him and gone off with a 'rich man'. When asked where Geraldine was, he said he didn't know.

'Stop asking me questions!' he snapped.

His uncle told him firmly that Beryl was not that sort of girl. With that, Evans got up and stormed out of the house into the street.

He walked about, until he ended up in a cafe near to the police station in Merthyr Tydfil.

He sat there for a while, considering his options. Then he headed into the station itself.

The long arm of the law would never let go.

Chapter 11
The Police Interviews

Timothy John Evans finished his coffee in the cafe at Merthyr Tydfil. He had a lot on his mind. He also had a lot of stories to tell officers at the police station, just along from the cafe.

He walked into the police station just after lunchtime on Wednesday, 30 November 1949. He was greeted by his namesake, Detective Constable Gwynfryn Howell Evans.

'Can I help you?'

Timothy Evans asked if there was someone of senior rank around, but there wasn't. So he said he wanted to talk to the detective constable alone.

They went through to the charge office, where he made an immediate confession.

'I want to give myself up. I've disposed of my wife.'

Naturally, the detective constable was taken aback, and keen to find out more details from this unexpected arrival at the police station.

'I put her down the drain,' Evans blurted out.

Evans was possibly remembering Christie's talk of putting Beryl's body down a manhole at the front of the house. He grasped at this to divert the police from where the bodies really lay, in the wash house.

The detective constable needed some assistance to deal with this remarkable development, and he found Detective Sergeant Glyndwr Gough in the recreation room. The two officers went back to the charge office, where Evans was waiting patiently to provide more information.

Detective Sergeant Gough said to Evans: 'I understand that you have told this officer that you have disposed of your wife's body by putting it down a drain in London, and that you wish to make a statement about it.'

After Evans had been cautioned, he said: 'Yes that's right. I want to get it off my chest.'

And so he made his first of many statements:

'About the beginning of October my wife, Beryl Susan Evans, told me that she was expecting a baby. She told me that she was about three months gone. I said, "If you are having a baby, well, you've had one, another won't make any difference." She then told me she was going to try and get rid of it. I turned round and told her not to be silly, that she'd make herself ill.

'Then she bought herself a syringe and started syringing herself. She said that didn't work, and I said, "I'm glad it won't work." Then she said she was going to buy some tablets. I don't know what tablets she bought because she was always hiding them from me. She started to look very ill, and I told her to go and see a doctor, and she said she'd go when I was in work, but when I'd come home and ask her if she'd been, she'd always say that she hadn't.

'On the Sunday morning, that would be 6 November, she told me that if she couldn't get rid of the baby, she'd kill herself and our other baby Geraldine. I told her she was talking silly. She never said no more about it then, but when I got up Monday morning to go to work she said she was going to see some woman to see if she could help her. Who the woman was she didn't tell me, and that if she wasn't in when I came home, she'd be up at her grandmother's.

'Then I went to work. I loaded up my van and went on my journey. About nine o'clock that morning I pulled up at a transport cafe between Ipswich and Colchester. I can't say exactly where it is, that's the nearest I can give. I went up to the counter and ordered a cup of tea and breakfast, and I sat down by the table with my cup of tea waiting for my breakfast to come up, and there was a man sitting by the table opposite me.

'He asked me if I had a cigarette I could give him. I gave him one and he started talking about married life. He said to me, "You are looking pretty worried, is there anything on your mind?" Then I told him all about it. So he said, "Don't let that worry you. I can give you something that can fix it." So he said, "Wait there a minute, I'll be back," and he went outside.

'When he came back he handed me a little bottle that was wrapped in brown paper. He said, "Tell your wife to take it first thing in the morning before she has any tea, then to lay down on the bed for a couple of hours and that should do the job." He never asked no money for it. I went up to the counter and paid my bill and carried on with my journey.

'After I finished my work I went home, that would be between seven and eight. When I got in the house I took off my overcoat and hung it on the peg behind the kitchen door. My wife asked me for a cigarette and I told her that there was one in my pocket, then she found this bottle in my pocket, and I told her all about it.

'I got up in the morning as usual at six o'clock to go to work. I made myself a cup of tea and made a feed for the baby. I told her not to take that stuff when I went in and said good morning to her, and I went to work, that would be about half past six. I finished work and got home about half past six in the evening.

'I then noticed that there was no lights in the place. I lit the gas and it started to go out, and I went into the bedroom to get a penny and I noticed my baby in the cot. I put the penny in the gas and went back in the bedroom and lit the gas in the bedroom. Then I saw my wife laying in the bed. I spoke to her but she never answered me, so I went over and shook her, then I could see she wasn't breathing. Then I went and made some food for my baby. I fed my baby and I sat up all night.

'Between about one and two in the morning I got my wife downstairs through the front door. I opened the drain outside my front door, that is No. 10 Rillington Place, and pushed her body head first into the drain. I closed the drain, then I went back in the house. I sat down by the fire smoking a cigarette. I never went to work the following day. I went and got my baby looked after.

'Then I went and told my governor where I worked that I was leaving. He asked me the reason, and I told him I had a better job elsewhere. I had my cards and money that afternoon, then I went to see a man about selling my furniture. The man came down and had a look at my furniture and he offered me £40 for it. So I accepted the £40.

'He told me he wouldn't be able to collect the furniture until Monday morning. In the meanwhile I went and told Mother that my wife and baby had gone for a holiday. I stopped in the flat till Monday. The van came Monday afternoon and cleared the stuff out. He paid me the money. Then I caught the five to one train from Paddington and I come down to Merthyr Vale and I've been down here ever since. That's the lot.'

It was quite a story from Timothy Evans. It was lies all the way, even down to the part about Beryl asking for a cigarette; she had never smoked in her life. He even got her middle name wrong. Naturally the Merthyr police called their colleagues at Notting Hill to check out the drain in Rillington Place.

And so the Notting Hill station sent officers round for a look. They saw a manhole outside No. 10. The cover was quite a weight, and it took three of them to lift it off. Inside, of course, there was no body.

Christie could see what was happening from his front window, and began formulating stories of his own. He knew he was becoming implicated in Beryl's death. The message from Notting Hill to Merthyr came back: 'We found nothing.'

At around 9pm, Detective Constable Evans relayed the news to the suspect down in Wales: the drain was empty.

He had been at the police station for six hours, no doubt mentally exhausted and wondering if any part of his statement could be believed. The story about the body down the drain was a non-starter as far as Detective Constable Evans was concerned.

'Well, I put it there,' was all the suspect could say when faced with the reality that there was no body down the drain.

He had obviously never studied the manhole, because he maintained that he managed to lift the cover off himself. Detective Constable Evans assured him that it was not a one-man job; three officers were needed to carry out the lifting and inspect the drain. So why did he lie about Beryl's body being down there?

'I said that to protect a man named Christie. It's not true about the man in the cafe either. I'll tell you the truth now.'

Detective Constable Evans prepared for the next instalment, and Timothy Evans was soon in full flow again.

'As I was coming home from work one night, that would be about a week before my wife died, Reg Christie who lived on the ground floor below us approached me and said, "I'd like to have a chat with you about your wife taking these tablets."'

Evans said that Christie knew what she was taking them for: to get rid of the baby. Christie told him they should have come to him in the first place. He could have done it for them without any risk. Evans said he told Christie that he was unaware of the medical knowledge.

'So he told me then that he was training for a doctor before the war. Then he started showing me books and things on medical. I was just as wise because I couldn't understand one word of it because I couldn't read. Then he told me that, with the stuff that he used, one out of every 10 would die with it. I told him that I was not interested, so I said good night to him and I went upstairs.

'When I got in, my wife started talking to me about it. She said that she had been speaking to Mr Christie and asked if he had spoken to me. I said, "Yes," and I told her what he had spoke to me about. I turned round and told her that I told him I didn't want nothing to do with it, and I told her she wasn't to have anything to do with it either. She turned round and told me to mind my own business and that she intended to get rid of it and she trusted Mr Christie. She said he could do the job without any trouble at all.

'On the Monday evening, that was 7 November, when I came home from work, my wife said that Mr Christie had made arrangements for first thing Tuesday morning. I didn't argue with her, I just washed and changed and went to the KPH (a public house) until 10 o'clock. I came home and had supper and went to bed. She wanted to start an argument but I just took no notice.'

Evans said he got up just after 6am on the Tuesday to go to work. He had a cup of tea and a smoke. He said Beryl told him to let Christie know on the way down that everything was all right. If he didn't tell him, she would speak to him herself. So he went downstairs and Christie appeared. Evans confirmed that everything was all right, and then went to work.

'When I came home in the evening he was waiting for me at the bottom of the staircase. He said, "Go on upstairs, I'll come behind you." When I lit the gas in the kitchen he said, "It's bad news. It didn't work." I asked him where was she. He said, "Laying on the bed in the bedroom." Then I asked him where was the baby. So he said, "The baby's in the cot." So I went into the bedroom, I lit the gas then I saw the curtains had been drawn. I looked at my wife and saw that she was covered with the eiderdown.'

Evans said he pulled the eiderdown back to have a look at Beryl, and saw immediately that she was dead. She was bleeding from the mouth and nose and also 'bleeding from the bottom part'. She was wearing a black skirt, checked blouse and light blue jacket.

'Christie was in the kitchen. I went over and picked up my baby. I wrapped the baby in a blanket and took her in the kitchen. In the meanwhile Mr Christie had lit the fire in the kitchen. He said, "I'll speak to you after you feed the baby." So I made the baby some tea and boiled an egg for her, then I changed the baby and put her to sit in front of the fire. Then I asked him how long my wife had been dead. He said, "Since about three o'clock." Then he told me that my wife's stomach was septic poisoned. He said, "Another day and she'd have gone to hospital." I asked him what he had done, but he wouldn't tell me.

'He then told me to stop in the kitchen and he closed the door and went out. He came back about a quarter of an hour later and told me that he had forced the door of Mr Kitchener's flat and had put my wife's body in there.'

Evans claimed he had asked Christie what he intended to do with the body and Christie said: 'I'll dispose of it down one of the drains.' Evans said he was instructed by Christie to go to work as usual in the morning, and he would get someone to look after the baby. In his statement, Evans also claimed he had told Christie it would be foolish to try to dispose of the body. But Christie feared getting into trouble with the police if he didn't dispose of Beryl.

'I got up next morning about six o'clock. I made myself a cup of tea and made the baby some breakfast and fed her and changed her and put her back into her cot. Christie had told me that he was going to look after the baby that day so I went to work. I saw Christie before I went and he told me that he would slip up and feed the baby during the day. I had wanted to take the baby to Mother the night before, but he said not to as it would cause suspicion straight away. He also told me in the morning that he knew a couple over in East Acton who would look after the baby, and he'd go over and see them.'

Evans went on to say that, when he got home from work on the Wednesday evening at about five or six, Christie had news for him. The young couple from East Acton would come on Thursday to take the baby. Evans's instructions were to feed and dress Geraldine, pack some clothes, and leave her in the cot. The couple would be arriving just after 9am to collect her.

'At half past five that evening I came home. I went upstairs and as I got in the kitchen he came up behind me. He told me that the people had called and took the baby with them, and to pack the rest of her things, and he had a case and would take them over to East Acton with the pram and her chair later in the week. I then asked him, how did he dispose of my wife's body. He said he put it down one of the drains. That's all he said to me, then he went downstairs. Later that evening I went around to see my mother, Mrs Thomasina Probert, at No. 11 St Mark's Road, London, W11.

'She asked me where Beryl and the baby was. I told her they had gone away on a holiday. When I left my mother's place that night I went up to the KPH to have a drink.

'I didn't go to work on the Friday as I had finished there on the Thursday. On that Thursday evening Christie said, "Now the best thing you can do is to sell your furniture and get out of London somewhere." I just said all right.

'On the Friday I went up to see a man in Portobello Road about selling my furniture. He came down on the Friday afternoon and said it was worth £40. He told me he would pick it up on the following Monday. On the Friday I went to the pictures and the pub, then went home to sleep. On the Saturday I did the same thing.

'On Sunday afternoon I went to see a rag dealer. I met him outside a cafe in Ladbroke Grove, that's where he lives. I told him that if he came down to my place on the Monday there was quite a lot of rags he could have.'

Evans said he got up at about 6am on the Monday morning and ripped up his wife's clothes. He also cut up the blanket. The rag dealer came round just after 9am and took about two full sacks. No money exchanged hands.

'About three o'clock the furniture van came. They cleared all the furniture out, and the bed clothes and lino, and the furniture man paid me £40 which I signed for. The only things left in the house then was vases, a clock, some dishes, saucepans and a bucket, and the case with the baby's clothes, her pram and small chair.'

Christie asked where he was going and Evans said he didn't know. He sorted out his case, took it to Paddington and left it in the left luggage department to be picked up later.

'I went to the pictures and a pub, and then I went to Paddington again and picked up my case about half-past twelve that evening and caught the five to one train to Cardiff. I got to Merthyr Vale about twenty to seven in the morning, then went to 93 Mount Pleasant, and I've been there ever since.'

The phone line from Merthyr to Notting Hill was buzzing again after the suspect's latest version of events. Officers from the two stations talked into the early hours of the morning, because the new Evans statement wasn't completed until just before midnight. There was also a message from Evans to his mother, Mrs Probert, that had to be relayed. He wanted her to find out from Christie about the couple in East Acton who were supposed to be looking after Geraldine.

An hour or so later, two officers went to her house in St Mark's Road to deliver that message and ask a few questions. Mrs Probert told them she had received a letter from her sister-in-law, Mrs Lynch, confirming that Evans had been staying there. Mrs Probert hadn't seen the baby or Beryl for a month. They were on holiday in Brighton with Beryl's father, she told the officers, although Dad had said that wasn't the case.

Mr and Mrs Lynch had to be awoken too, in the early hours. Officers went to see them, knowing that Mrs Probert had told Notting Hill police that her son was a terrible liar with a vivid imagination. Having heard about his statements made at Merthyr, they knew that already.

The Lynches told the Merthyr officers everything they knew, covering his arrival and what had gone on. They also had the letter from Mrs Probert; it was handed over to the police.

The Merthyr officer who had interviewed Evans at the start of all this wanted to ask more questions. Around mid-morning they had another chat. Did he know about the letter from Mrs Probert? It had been placed on the mantelpiece. Evans said he did know about the letter, but not its contents.

Detective Constable Evans, obviously a lot sharper than his namesake, wanted to dig for more information. As the theory about the drain had been discounted, he wanted to know when Evans had last seen Beryl's body. Had he been involved in moving my sister somewhere? Evans said he saw the body shortly before Christie took it to the flat occupied by Mr Kitchener, who was presumably in hospital at the time.

His story went that he heard Christie blowing and puffing and saw him halfway down to Mr Kitchener's place. He was struggling to get Beryl's body downstairs.

Evans said he asked Christie what was wrong, and he was told that he couldn't manage it alone. Christie asked Evans to pick up her legs so that they could get Beryl into the flat on the first floor.

'I picked up her legs and carried her into Kitchener's place with him.'

Evans also admitted going back to London, claiming he wanted to find out how Geraldine was getting on in East Acton. He said Christie believed it was too early to see his daughter.

Evans stated that he had cut up Beryl's clothes with scissors and his hands. And he maintained that, although some of his stories didn't add up, the parts about Christie were true.

Back in Notting Hill, it was time to have a look around 10 Rillington Place. The police were not sure whether they were looking for a body, a missing person, two bodies or two missing people. Reg Christie was incredibly tense as police looked round the garden. It certainly wasn't good for his diarrhoea.

The police found a stolen briefcase and a newspaper cutting in Evans's flat. The cutting was all about the murder of Stanley Setty, known as a dodgy car dealer from the East End of London who had vanished the previous month, on 4 October 1949. An equally dodgy business partner, Donald Hume, was charged with his murder.

They found nothing else of real significance during that initial search.

However, one thing was certain.

They would return.

Chapter 12
Bodies in the Wash House

The police checks on the whereabouts of Beryl and Geraldine had drawn a blank. They were not in Bristol, and had never arrived in Brighton. Another search of Rillington Place was required, and it took place on 2 December 1949.

Detective Chief Inspector George Jennings took charge of the Notting Hill operation. A visit to 10 Rillington Place was planned involving Jennings, Detective Chief Superintendent Thomas Barratt and a pathologist from Scotland Yard.

Christie, as usual, answered the front door and invited them, in his whispery voice, to come inside. During this search, they carried out an in-depth inspection of Christie's flat. Their mission was to find out if any equipment, used to carry out abortions, existed.

They searched everywhere throughout the building and found nothing.

They were also interested in the wash house and garden, and went straight through. They found that the wash house door wouldn't open. That was a regular problem, said Mrs Christie, and she went off to retrieve a piece of metal to help them open it. That would do the trick, she said.

This was a moment of panic for Christie. How could he create a diversionary tactic? He walked around outside, holding his back. Perhaps inviting some sympathy might slow down the search or distract the officers. Undeterred, Jennings and his colleagues carried on with their business.

Thanks to Ethel, the door was opened, and the officers shone a torch inside. To their left was a device known as a copper, consisting of a cauldron with a lid and a space underneath for a fire to heat water. A chimney went up through the top of the wash house. Beside the copper was a sink and tap. A stack of wood was piled up against the sink, which looked rather odd. They removed the wood and explored behind the timbers.

The officers' torches shed light on a package in a dark coloured blanket, tied up with cord.

'Do you know what this is, Mrs Christie?'

'I'm sorry, I've no idea. I didn't know anything was in there.'

The policemen pulled out the bulky package and laid it outside the wash house. No one said a word. Experience told the assembled group what was wrapped inside.

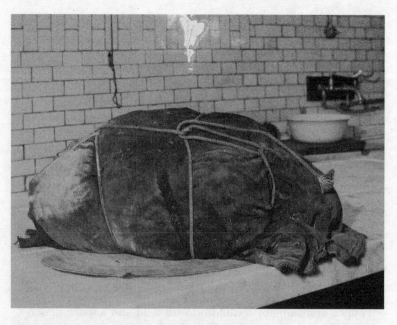

Above: The body of Beryl after being tied up by Christie.
Below: Beryl's body at Kensington Borough Mortuary.

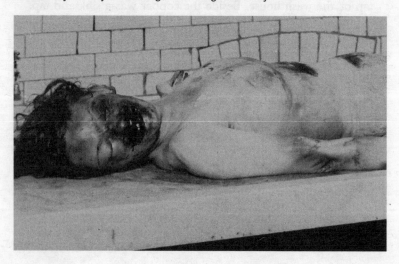

Behind the wash house door lay a few strips of wood. The officers removed the wood and were shocked to discover the body of Geraldine, with the tie still tight around her neck.

At that moment, everything changed. The officers' moods became dark and severe, and they needed back-up. They made an urgent call to Home Office pathologist Dr Donald Teare, who quickly arrived on the scene. The evidence was intact, and Dr Teare arranged for the grim finds to be taken to the local mortuary.

At the mortuary, the blanket covering Beryl was taken off. There had been no alert in the neighbourhood of any smell, because of the cold November weather. It was as if the bodies had been refrigerated. Beryl and Geraldine, Dr Teare concluded, had been in the wash house for three weeks or so. It was clear that the woman and child had been strangled.

Dr Teare could see that Beryl had substantial facial injuries. She had severe bruising to her throat and neck, while there was swelling to her top lip and right eye. He noticed bruises inside her vagina, possibly caused by Beryl trying to self-abort.

Beryl was wearing a black skirt, spotted cotton blouse and light blue woollen jacket. Geraldine was said to be wearing normal clothing for a baby girl of 13 months old.

Back at Rillington Place, Christie skulked around in the garden, looking shocked and continuing to hold his painful back. He could only pace up and down, fearful of what was going to happen next.

Evans was still down in Merthyr. Detective Inspector James Black and Detective Sergeant Corfield travelled to Wales by train, with orders to detain Evans on a holding charge relating to a stolen briefcase. They left Merthyr in the afternoon, with instructions not to discuss the murder inquiry with Evans.

On the way back they talked about trivial matters, including the fortunes of Evans's favourite football club, Queens Park Rangers. At around 9.30pm, the three arrived at Paddington, where they were met by Chief Inspector Jennings, and they travelled by car to the police station at Notting Hill.

To prepare for his arrival, the police had arranged two sets of clothing side by side. The tie, used to strangle Geraldine, lay on top of the baby's clothes.

'I am Chief Inspector Jennings, in charge of this case. At 11.50am today, I found the dead body of your wife Beryl Evans concealed in a wash house at 10 Rillington Place, Notting Hill, also the body of your baby daughter Geraldine in the same building, and this clothing was found on them. Later this day I was present at Kensington Mortuary where it was established the cause of death was strangulation in both cases. I have reason to believe that you were responsible for their deaths.'

As I've said, Evans was a man who bragged non-stop, and talked nonsense a lot of the time. But on this occasion, all he could say was 'Yes'.

He was cautioned and made yet another statement.

'She was incurring one debt after another and I could not stand it any longer, so I strangled her with a piece of rope and took her down to the flat below the same night whilst the old man was in hospital. I waited till the Christies downstairs had gone to bed, then I took her to the wash house after midnight. This was on Tuesday, 8 November. On Thursday evening, after I came home from work, I strangled my baby in our bedroom with my tie and later that night I took her down into the wash house after the Christies had gone to bed.'

There was no way Evans could have placed the bodies in the wash house during the week, because the builders were still active in and out of 10 Rillington Place.

Evans knew too much about the killings for an innocent man. He was volunteering information about where the bodies were and how his wife and daughter had been strangled, without the police having to give him the details.

He made yet another statement after this one. He was giving version after version of events, with contradictions all over the place. Yet he did seem to have knowledge that only the killer could have.

While Evans was in his cell early on 3 December, an officer questioned him on the circumstances surrounding the deaths. The murder of a baby seemed incomprehensible.

'It was the constant crying of the baby that got on my nerves. I just had to strangle it. I had to put an end to it. I just couldn't put up with its crying.'

That day, Timothy Evans was formally charged with murdering my niece.

The workmen were asked about their movements in and out of the wash house, but their record of dates at the time was all over the place, with missing timesheets. I had seen them coming and going when I made my final visit to Beryl.

The plasterer, Frederick Willis, said he finished the ceiling of the wash house about mid-morning on Wednesday, 9 November. He said he was constantly in and out of the building until he left the job on 11 November. After more police questioning, Mr Willis said it was possible that anything could have been placed behind the timbers under the sink.

Plasterer's mate Frederick Jones told police that wooden shores were put up while the work was being carried out, so the wash house was more or less sealed off.

'All the time we were there, I saw nothing at all in the wash house other than the materials we were using and our tools. After completing the work on Friday afternoon, 11 November, I personally swept out the wash house and also cleaned out the copper which was in it. There was definitely nothing in the wash house or the copper.'

Oddly, the date for the sweeping out was later changed to the Tuesday. He said he just collected all the tools without paying particular attention to the wash house. Another section of a statement from Frederick Jones read as follows:

'At about 10am on Wednesday, 9 November 1949, I was mixing up materials outside 10 Rillington Place, W11. With the front door open, I saw a young woman come downstairs with a baby in her arms and she was accompanied by another young woman. She put the baby in a pram, which was already outside the front door, and I said to her, "Mind how you go when you come back, as I am going to lay a ladder up the stairs." She replied, "I'll get by that alright." I did not pay any particular attention to this woman or her companion, and could not recognise them again. Apart from saying the woman with the baby was small and thin, I cannot further describe her. This was the first and last time I saw these people.'

The woman with the baby had to be Joan Vincent, accompanied by one of her friends. The other person could have been Lucy Endicott or even Evans's sister, Maureen.

The date was later changed, again, to Tuesday, 8 November. It seems to me that the stories had to fit in with the beliefs of DCI Jennings who was apparently determined to make everything fit perfectly with the case that he was building. I cannot see how any of the statements by the workmen can be relied upon, as I suspect they were later manipulated into changing their versions.

One thing is certain: that sighting could not have been as early as Monday, 7 November, when Beryl was still alive. For a start, it was raining and there were no workmen that day.

From the police station, Evans was taken to Brixton prison where, in the hospital wing, he had his pre-trial medical check-up.

There he met Donald Hume, the convicted murderer of Stanley Setty, and Evans knew all about that case from the newspaper cutting in 10 Rillington Place.

Evans was interested in Hume, and the police were interested in what had drawn Evans to his case.

Evans certainly knew the background to the Hume murder case. Stan 'The Spiv' Setty sold cars by the kerbside in Warren Street, a couple of minutes' walk from Euston Square. The deals were all in cash, as gullible buyers were tempted by shiny new motors with hidden histories, clocks turned back and chunks of filler holding them together. Gangland enforcer Frankie Fraser described the buyers as 'mug punters', with people coming from as far away as Scotland, only to be ripped off by the spivs.

Hume and Setty had one thing in common: they both liked to make lots of money dealing in the black market. As well as stolen cars for Setty to spray a different colour and sell on, there were nylons, forged petrol coupons and all sort of goods that were difficult to find in those days.

The pair became involved in a fierce argument at Hume's flat in Finchley Road. The row was believed to be over Hume's dog marking one of Setty's newly resprayed motors. Hume grabbed a German SS dagger, hanging on the wall, and plunged it repeatedly into Setty's ribs. Hume carved the body up, wrapped the parts in parcels, hired a light aircraft and dumped the remains out over the English Channel. Unfortunately for Hume, some of the body parts floated back into the Essex Marshes.

Evans was totally fascinated by the case and the story about the German dagger. He could never have imagined he would be in the same prison hospital as Hume. He knew all about the torso case.

Describing prison life, Evans said: 'We play dominoes and games of all kinds all day, but you have to watch Hume.'

Hume told Evans he should not confess to the murders of Beryl and Geraldine, telling him: 'Don't stick your neck in a noose.'

Evans was also advised by Hume to appear 'more dense than he was'. Hume said Evans should play on the fact he was illiterate, and claim that he didn't understand the police methods of taking statements and that his confessions were not true.

Later, Hume said he was unimpressed when Evans revealed why he had killed Geraldine. 'In the presence of several prisoners, Evans admitted to killing the baby because it kept crying. So in the presence of these lags and a guard, I hooked him and was booked for it. I have no scruples about adults killing each other, but I dislike people who hurt kids and animals.'

That is not uncommon in prisons, especially with gangland figures. They give child killers and sex offenders a hard time, so it was no surprise that Evans was 'hooked', especially as Hume's wife, Cynthia, had recently given birth to a little girl.

Back in Notting Hill, there was an unsettling mood at 10 Rillington Place. Reg Christie's dog Judy had dug up a skull in the back garden around the time of the police search. Christie, however, managed to dispose of it unnoticed.

Christie took the skull to a bombed-out house nearby, beside the tennis courts in St Mark's Road, and dropped it inside. Bodies from the wartime air raids were still being discovered all the time in the rubble in Notting Hill, so for the moment, Christie was safe and free of suspicion.

Evans, on the other hand, was in deep trouble. He looked as guilty as a man could ever be.

Chapter 13
Letter to New Zealand

My unwanted sea journey to New Zealand had got off to a good start. It was plain sailing all the way down under. We stopped at Curaçao, then the Panama Canal, before setting off from there all the way across the Pacific Ocean. It took five weeks and four days, all in all.

They fed us good meals. The children didn't go into the main dining room with the fee-paying passengers; there was a separate room for us to eat in. Each cabin had room for two or three boys, and it was the same for the girls. I made some friends, although I never saw any of them after the voyage.

When I arrived, I worked on a farm at the top of the North Island, miles from anywhere. I worked from seven in the morning until seven at night, milking cows, looking after racehorses, and receiving hearty meals to keep me going through the day. I told the family I was staying with all about Beryl and Geraldine – how worried I was about them and how much I was looking forward to seeing them again.

Before long, I worked my way south and got a job with a dry-cleaning firm, before starting work at another farm, staying with a couple called the Mansons. Mr and Mrs Manson were a normal farming couple, middle-aged, usually dressed in tough outdoor wear for their work. It was a lonely life: there was me, the two of them and one Maori worker at the farm, and that was it. They did at least have a collection of friendly farm dogs and one or two cats.

One morning the Mansons received their post as usual, and Mr Manson told me there was a letter for me. Oddly, it had Mr Manson's name on the envelope, but I was delighted nonetheless – a letter from home! How was everyone getting on? How were Beryl and Geraldine?

I was excited to see Dad's handwriting again, and smiled at the Mansons. There were two letters inside the envelope, one for them and one for me. Mr Manson held one and gave the other to me. I grinned with glee.

He didn't smile back. Instead, he looked down at the floor.

That struck me as peculiar. I sat down at the kitchen table and started to read.

The contents of the letter, and the news relayed by the Mansons, have stayed with me ever since.

Letter to New Zealand

Jan 11th, 1950
10 Chapel St, Brighton

My Dear Peter,

Just a few lines to say how pleased we all are to know that you are so happy in your new home. I expect you are getting as big as a house and growing tall. I shall always have the pleasure of looking up to my son. Thanks for the snaps, Peter, we all think they are lovely and you look ever so tall. Of course, it is the good food, lovely fresh air and new surroundings. We all enjoyed the show at the Hip, but we missed your face. We have all been to see 'The Sleeping Beauty', the Christmas pantomime, which was very good. Pat and Basil are keeping very well.

Now Peter, I want you to be a man like your Dad, as I have some very bad news for you. At the moment, this is a very sad house indeed, but we are all bearing up under the strain as best we can. I'm afraid the worst has fallen on me as I have got to answer all the questions. Had it not been for Mum, I don't know what would have happened to me. I am enclosing a letter to Mr and Mrs Manson, asking them to break the news to you as best they can.

I must draw this letter to a close now, as I really don't feel well enough to write any more. You will understand my feelings when you know the news.

From your ever loving Dad

    PS Mum and Pat send their fondest love to you and hope that you will be a man to hear the bad news.

xxxxxxxxxxx

God bless and stay safe in His keeping.

Mr Manson broke the grim news as gently as he could.

I don't know if the letter contained graphic details, but he managed to tell me that Beryl and Geraldine had been found at 10 Rillington Place under difficult circumstances. I read between the lines and Mr and Mrs Manson put their arms around me.

Of course, the 'Mum' he refers to is Marguerita. I had already told the Mansons that our own mother died in 1947. Oh, how we hated this awful new woman in his life being described as 'Mum'.

I cried and cried. I wept until no more tears could come out.

I knew I had to get home somehow, as soon as possible. But where would I get the money? How could I return home?

I was in a daze. I went up to my room, took Beryl's wedding ring out of its safe place in a drawer, and gazed at it. For me, that was the only tangible connection I now had left with my sister. I remembered how she had given it to me with a look of despair and those sad, sad eyes. Memories flooded back of how she feared for her life; as I stood, weeping in my room, I knew for sure that Evans had killed Beryl and Geraldine. I cried my eyes out looking at that band of gold, knowing only too well what she would have gone through.

Beryl and Geraldine were gone, but I realised from that moment that my future was mapped out. I needed to find out exactly what had happened inside 10 Rillington Place.

I summoned up the courage to go back downstairs into the kitchen. Mr and Mrs Manson were a kindly couple, who really looked after me, and I could see they were upset. Mr Manson could never have imagined, when he took me on, that he would have to break the news about the murders of my sister and niece.

'Come and sit at the table.' Mrs Manson gestured, holding a teapot and a cup. 'You're a good lad. You don't deserve this.'

'I know who did it,' I said sternly. 'It was her husband. Beryl told me he had threatened to kill her.'

'Are you sure?' Mr Manson sort of gasped. 'Surely not her husband. I was thinking it was someone who carried out a random attack.'

The look on my face said it all. The Mansons realised then that I knew the identity of the killer, and that I was determined to get to the truth. I needed to get a plan in place.

My life, from that point onwards, would revolve around what really happened in 10 Rillington Place.

Chapter 14
The Case Against Evans

Two of the most well-respected experts at the time, Dr Donald Teare and Dr Francis Camps, wrote full pathology reports on Beryl and Geraldine, and the records still exist.

Dr Teare carried out autopsies on Beryl and Geraldine at Kensington Borough Mortuary, in addition to the earlier examination after the bodies' discovery. Both had been found fully clothed, with the exception that Beryl was not wearing knickers. The cause of death was confirmed as 'asphyxia due to strangulation by ligature' in both cases. It also showed that Beryl had been beaten up before death, causing a black eye and a bruised upper lip and nose, suggesting punches were probably thrown with a fist to the face. Dr Teare thought that the blows had been struck about 20 minutes before her death.

There was further bruising on her thigh and leg.

Dr Teare recorded results of the internal examination, where he noted 'two marks on the posterior wall of the vagina'. One appeared to be an old unrelated scar beside a small bruise. This bruise could have been the result of 'forced intercourse' or 'a struggle'. On reflection, it was most likely a direct result of a self-inflicted attempt to abort herself by the use of a syringe. She was, at this time, four months pregnant.

The full details from the post-mortem examination were as follows:

The external examination showed a series of abrasions, including a three-and-a-half-inch-long bruise on the right side of her throat, which varied from three eighths of an inch to one and a quarter inches wide.

On the left side at the back of the neck there were a group of abrasions, two and a half inches long by one and a quarter inches at the widest point. There was also a small abrasion three eighths of an inch in diameter to the left of the mid-line immediately above the collarbone. There was also a bruise one and a half inches in diameter on the inner part of the left thigh, four inches above the knee.

There was a bruise two and a half inches long by one inch wide on the inner area of the left calf, immediately below the knee.

In addition: severe swelling of the right eye and upper lip due to bruising, with haemorrhages evident on the right side and point of the chin. They were also found on the surfaces of the lungs and epiglottis, with deep bruising to the right side of the voice box.

The uterus contained a male foetus six and a quarter inches long, showing a length of pregnancy of about 16 weeks. The membranes were intact and that there was no evidence of interference.

The post-mortem examination also said: 'There were strong indications that Beryl had been strangled from behind and that some of the bruising around the throat suggested that she probably made a desperate grab at the ligature in an attempt to release it.'

The general conclusion was that she had been a healthy woman.

The external examination showed that Geraldine was 14 months old, and 33 and a half inches tall. The body was that of a well-nourished baby girl. She was dressed as normal for a child of her age. She was not wrapped up in anything.

A tie was found extremely tight around her neck. The circumference of the ligature was six and a half inches.

Haemorrhages were evident on areas of the heart and surfaces of the lungs, which were a little collapsed and very congested. The right side of the heart was widely dilated, but showed no evidence of congenital abnormalities or disease.

There was definite bruising in the muscles around the upper area of the voice box and the base of the tongue. The liver was congested and the stomach was empty. The general conclusion was: she had been a well-developed and perfectly healthy child.

The report is all correct, apart from the fact that they should have recorded Geraldine as 13 months old.

There were no traces of sperm to suggest that sexual intercourse had taken place either before or after death, although Dr Teare apparently did not take a swab at the time. But his professional integrity never came into question.

The case against Evans for the murder of Beryl was clear. But, in those days, a person could only be tried for one murder at a time. And so Evans could not face trial for the murders of Beryl and Geraldine at the same time. The prosecution was permitted to decide which one they wished to proceed with, and although Beryl had been murdered first, the prosecution decided to concentrate on the death of baby Geraldine: in the case of the murder of a child, there was no chance of a 'provocation and manslaughter' defence.

A medical report on Evans was submitted before the start of his trial by Dr John Matheson.

He said: 'My interviews with him [Evans] suggest that he has an inadequate psychopathic personality which, with his low intelligence, makes him less able to adjust himself satisfactorily to reality, and tends to make him act impulsively with little or no foresight or consideration for others.'

The next piece of crucial evidence against Evans is the statement made to police by Joan Vincent. It was taken by Detective Sergeant John Corfield, 'F' Division. Joan makes her feelings towards Evans very clear.

MRS JOAN FRANCES VINCENT, age 19, of 164 Westbourne Park, W11, states:

I am a married woman and live with my husband and child at the above address.

I have known Beryl Thorley since I was at school about seven years ago. We were always firm friends, but I did not go about with her a great deal after we left school.

Until Beryl got married about two years ago, she lived with her parents at Cambridge Gardens, W10. I cannot recall the number of the house. Her mother died whilst she was there. She married Tim Evans and they went to live with his mother at St Mark's Rd, W11. Later they moved to 10 Rillington Place, W11.

About 12 months ago I became very friendly with Mrs Evans again. She had a young baby at the time, and I was expecting my baby. I saw Mrs Evans fairly often, especially after I had my baby, and we used to visit each other's addresses three or four times a week. I have never had a quarrel with Mrs Evans, but I know that on occasions Mr Evans used to row with her, because she came to see me so often. Mr Evans was always all right to my face, but I never liked him. Beryl told me that her husband had been carrying on with a friend she had taken home from her work. He never made any advances to me and we never had an association of any description.

About a month ago I met Mrs Evans and she told me she was expecting another baby. I understand that, because of her living conditions and strained relationship with her husband, she did not want the baby. She told me all about the different things she was taking to bring about her miscarriage.

From what I could gather, the husband was not anxious that the child should be born. I went round to 10 Rillington Place, W11, to see Mrs Evans on Saturday, 5 November, to get back some tea which she had borrowed. I was only there for a few minutes and as I left I saw Mr Evans, her husband, drive his van up to the door. He smiled and said 'hello' to me, then went into the house. Shortly afterwards I met Mr Thorley, Beryl's father, walking down Rillington Place, W11.

I then returned to 10 Rillington Place, W11 and Beryl loaned me a shirt which I had arranged to borrow.

The last time I saw Beryl Evans was on Friday about three weeks ago. Mr Evans came up to my address at 164 Westbourne Park Road, W11. It would be about 5.45pm. I was surprised to see him, because I think he quarrelled with his wife over something I had told Beryl. He told me that Beryl had taken the child to some of his relatives at Bristol for a holiday and that she would be writing to me. Mr Evans only stayed about 20 minutes.

During the following week I again met Mr Evans on the corner of Lancaster Road and Ladbroke Grove. He said he had had a telegram from Beryl at Bristol, saying the baby was ill and he was going to catch a night train to Bristol.

I have not seen Mr Evans since this occasion and I have not received any letters or communication from Beryl. I know that they were in debt.

Beryl's brother, Basil, works at the Royalty cinema, Lancaster Road, W11, and I believe lives in a young man's hostel at the top of Portobello Road. Her father lives in Brighton. I understood that Mr and Mrs Evans were shortly to take a flat at Peabody Buildings, North Kensington. I know that Mr Evans is known in the locality to be a liar.

On 1 December 1949, in company with my husband, I was shown a brown leather briefcase with the initials 'JN' on the front in black letters.

I have been told that this case was stolen, together with a hand-made rug, from Mr Nicols's flat, which is on the same floor as ours at 164 Westbourne Park Road, W11, between 19 and 23 August this year. I certainly know nothing whatever about the theft of either the briefcase or the rug mentioned above.

This statement has been read by me and it is true.

FURTHER STATES:

When I made my previous statement I omitted that I had been to Beryl Evans's address after 5 November 1949. In fact, I had been along there twice after this date. Round about 10.30am on Monday, 7 November 1949, I called at 10 Rillington Place to see Beryl.

The front door was open and I went upstairs to Beryl's rooms. The kitchen door was shut. I thought I heard a movement in the kitchen and called out, 'Are you there, Beryl?' I did not receive a reply. I said, 'I am sure somebody is in there, and if you don't want to open the door, you needn't.'

I did not go to the front room, and went back downstairs, where I saw Mrs Christie in the hall. I told her that I thought there was something funny going on upstairs, as I couldn't get the kitchen door open and had a feeling that someone was inside. I asked her if she knew if someone was in, and she said she didn't know.

I left, saying I would come back another time. During lunch-time on Thursday, 10 November 1949, I went back to the house; the front door was open and I walked up the stairs to the second flight when Mr Christie came out and called, 'Who's there?' He was down in the hall.

I said, 'It's Joan. I want to see Beryl.'

Mr Christie said, 'She isn't here, she has gone away. I expect if she wants you, she will write to you.'

After some conversation I left and went back to work. When I was upstairs on these two occasions I did not hear any noise from the baby. I did not call round at 10 Rillington Place after this.

In August 1949, Lucy was staying with Beryl at 10 Rillington Place. One Sunday night in August 1949, my husband and I were walking home through St Mark's Road, and we saw Beryl, who informed me she was going for the police to get Lucy out.

Later that night I was talking to someone in St Mark's Road, when Lucy and Timothy Evans came along the road carrying Lucy's suitcases. They accompanied us to our flat when they told us she had had a row with Beryl and that police had been called there.

Tim and Lucy stayed at our house till about 11.00pm when I mentioned I was sorry I couldn't put them up, although they didn't ask us. They both left to get a room.

The next morning, Lucy came to see me and stayed the day. During the afternoon, Lucy and I met Evans and he took her away in the evening.

The following afternoon, I was in St Mark's Road and I saw Evans. He showed me a note which said, 'Sorry Tim I have gone home to Mother. It wouldn't work.' I think it was signed Lucy.

He asked me what I thought of it and I told him it was for the best and he should go back to his wife. After this he called here once or twice and saw Lucy, and I understand their friendship ceased.

This statement has been read over to me and it is true.

Statement taken by Chief Inspector Jennings, written down, read over and signature witnessed by James N. Black, Detective Inspector, 'F' Division.

When I saw Joan in Rillington Place, I could tell she was a normal, everyday girl, much the same as Beryl. I used to see the two of them sitting chatting in the flat upstairs with their babies, planning for the future and talking about schools for their children. Joan was already running around after a husband and young baby at the age of 19, so the murders of Beryl and Geraldine must have come as a horrible shock and placed even more strain on her. Joan did struggle with dates and events, as you can see.

The legal proceedings against Timothy Evans began in earnest on Thursday 15 December before West London Magistrates' Court. At the hearing, Evans was further charged with the murder of Beryl, to add to the charge of murdering Geraldine. Evans would face trial for Geraldine's murder first, and if he was found not guilty, only then would he face the charge of Beryl's murder.

The prosecutor, Maurice Crump, gave a resume of the case and how the bodies were found in the wash house. Christie was called; after saying he was unwell, he was given a seat in the courtroom. He described how he had heard a thud in the night on 8 November. His wife Ethel was also called, but she didn't have much to say because she was too upset about the whole affair.

Evans was remanded in custody, awaiting his trial.

One of the top reporters at the time was Harry Procter, who worked for *The Sunday Pictorial* and *The Daily Mail*. He visited Christie and was invited into 10 Rillington Place. He saw what I had seen so many times: the table and chairs in the kitchen, the dresser, the gas stove and the rope chair.

Procter recalled that Christie's smile was 'thin and suspicious'. His handshake was wet and limp.

They talked about the murders of Beryl and Geraldine, with Christie asking who might be responsible. Like me, Harry had a cup of tea – probably without the sticky buns and card games – and Christie complained about the intensive police operation. He wasn't getting any sleep.

Around this time, a skull was discovered around the corner at 133 St Mark's Road. It was the same skull Christie had dropped there. The coroner remarked that no one at that address had been unaccounted for after an air raid, and there was no link to any existing murder case either. Body parts and skulls were still being found after the wartime bombings, and that skull could simply have been yet another victim.

That skull would soon be identified as belonging to a woman named Muriel Eady.

Chapter 15
Christie the Star Witness

Timothy John Evans found No. 1 court at the Old Bailey a totally alien environment. He might as well have been transported onto the face of the moon. He was always uncomfortable in social situations, and now felt totally exposed before people who were far more intelligent than him. Evans was like a fish out of water, surrounded by barristers in gowns and wigs, and faced with Mr Justice Lewis in all his robes and finery.

He was in awe as he studied his surroundings. The legal costumes and lavish surroundings oozed elegance and a rich history.

In later years, Ronnie and Reggie Kray and the Yorkshire Ripper, Peter Sutcliffe, would be judged in the same courtroom.

It would not have helped Evans to know that Newgate Prison was situated next to the original Old Bailey courthouse. Six hundred executions had taken place there between 1783 and 1799, and an even greater number in the 1800s. Many of the hangings were carried out in public, with thousands of people jostling for position to enjoy the main entertainment of the day. A massive rebuilding project followed, and the lavish new court complex was opened by King Edward VII in 1907.

The courtroom is dominated by the dock. At 16ft by 14ft, it is enormous. The surroundings consist of a mix of expensive-looking leather and wood. The defendant looks straight at the judge, at around the same eye level, at a distance of about 25ft.

Evans was looking straight at Mr Justice Lewis – full title Sir Wilfred Hubert Poyer Lewis. A British judge, barrister and ecclesiastical lawyer, he was called to the Bar in 1908, with his first practice in Cardiff. He was commissioned into Glamorgan Yeomanry in the First World War, being mentioned in dispatches twice and awarded the OBE.

The senior Counsel to the Crown was Mr Christmas Humphreys. As a prosecutor, he had already worked on many notable cases. He was involved in the 'Tokyo trial' between 1946 and 1948, when 28 Japanese military and political leaders were charged with war crimes. Sentences ranged from prison terms to execution. In later years Humphreys was also the prosecutor who built up evidence against Ruth Ellis, who shot her lover, racing driver David Blakely, outside a London pub in 1955.

Humphreys announced that he would be proving the charge that the defendant, Evans, had murdered his daughter, Geraldine. As I pointed out, only a single case could be dealt with at any one time, and Humphreys chose the charge of Geraldine's murder over Beryl's. His reasoning was clear: there could be few explanations for Geraldine's killing other than murder; as I mentioned earlier, the baby could hardly have provoked Evans, so manslaughter was unlikely.

Mr Justice Lewis, however, decided that the death of Beryl was relevant to the case, so he allowed evidence about her killing to be presented.

Evans pleaded not guilty to the murder charge.

Mr Humphreys had been preparing the prosecution case for the case against Donald Hume in the Stanley Setty 'torso murder' case. It must have played on his mind, given the massive public interest in the Hume case and all its complexities. He wanted to get the Evans trial over and done with as soon as possible.

The evidence of identification was given from my father's earlier statement: 'Beryl Susanna Thorley was my daughter. She was aged 20 and married to the defendant. I last saw her on 5 November 1949. On 3 December 1949, at Kensington Mortuary, I identified the body of my daughter Beryl and that of my granddaughter Geraldine, who was about 14 months old, to Chief Inspector Jennings and Inspector Black.'

It is odd that this statement was read out in court, rather than my father being called as a witness. It is recorded that he was 'bound over' at the time, but we have no idea what his offence was. After all, he was one of the last people to see Beryl alive. His evidence, about seeing Beryl on the Saturday, and the reason he was there, could have been crucial. He could have told the court about her fears, what had happened in the house, and why he didn't take Beryl and Geraldine to Brighton with him. The effect of all this trauma haunted my father and probably explains why his behaviour became erratic.

Mr Humphreys concentrated on Evans's many inconsistent accounts of his actions. The prosecutor said it was a 'terrible accusation' that he had initially made against Christie, pinning responsibility for the deaths on him. Mr Humphreys noted, though, that Evans had then changed his mind and confessed to the murders of his wife and baby.

'You will listen to the evidence of the witnesses for the prose-cution,' Mr Humphreys told the jury, 'and you will listen to any evidence which the accused may put forward through his counsel or by any other witnesses he may call, but when you have heard all of the evidence you may well think – and indeed, you must be certain in your minds that it is so – that he murdered this baby, and in that case, you will find him guilty of wilful murder.'

Quite incredibly, Joan Vincent wasn't called as a witness at the trial, despite having given so much crucial background infor-mation in her statement that could have been useful to the court.

The star witness for the prosecution was John Reginald Halliday Christie, who recalled hearing a 'very loud thud' during the night of 8 November. He said he knew nothing about the movement of the body, though many in the court suspected that Evans would have needed help to move Beryl.

The prosecution wanted to build up Christie as a man of good character and an upstanding citizen; the defence team did their best to discredit him, to deflect attention away from Evans. Malcolm Morris QC, defending Evans, went on the offensive about the noises in the night. 'What, I am suggesting to you, happened then, is that you carried the dead body of Mrs Evans, with Evans's help, down to Kitchener's flat that evening.'

Christie said the idea that he had assisted Evans was 'absolutely ridiculous' and completely false.

Humphreys, for the prosecution, defended Christie's character by emphasising his service during the First World War. Christie had been gassed during the fighting, lost his voice for three and a half years, and was blinded for three months; during the Second World War, he served in the War Reserve Police the court was told. Christie was keen to mention that he was commended twice for his work during the blackout years. It was true that he had been in trouble with the police in the past, but that was a long time ago.

Evans's lawyer Morris, who had been made aware of Christie's dodgy record before the trial started, went on the attack.

'On four occasions, you have been convicted of offences of dishonesty…'

'Three.'

'Not four?'

'No.'

Morris mentioned the imprisonment for stealing postal orders in 1921.

'Yes, I remember that,' said Christie.

'Bound over for false pretences in 1923 in Halifax?'

'Yes, I remember that.'

'Nine months' hard labour for stealing material and goods in 1924 in Uxbridge?'

'Yes.'

Morris chipped in with the theft of a car, and Christie admitted to it.

Morris pointed out that he had mentioned four offences and Christie said he had thought it was only three. The barrister was about to play what he thought was his trump card.

'What is perhaps more important and relevant to this matter: is there another conviction recorded against you?'

'Yes.'

'And is that for malicious wounding, for which you were sentenced to six months' imprisonment in 1929?'

Christie had no choice but to admit that one too. Morris tried hard to turn the tables on him.

'Mr Christie, I have got to suggest to you, and I don't want there to be any misapprehension about this, that you are responsible for the death of Mrs Evans and the little girl; or, if that is not so, at least that you know very much more about those deaths than you have said?'

'That is a lie!'

Christie protested his innocence in no uncertain terms. He may not have killed either my sister or niece, but he certainly had plenty of knowledge about the deaths. Really, he knew everything.

Humphreys, in turn, found a weakness in Evans's defence to exploit: how could anyone know whether Evans was telling the truth?

'You lied to the Christies, did you not, that your wife was away, and all the rest of it, did you not?'

'I lied to Mrs Christie, yes.'

'You lied to your aunt down in Wales, Mrs Lynch, did you not?'

'Yes, sir.'

'So you lied to Mrs Christie, your aunt, the police and to your boss?'

'Yes, I did it all on the advice of Mr Christie.'

Humphreys had his man. 'All on the advice of Mr Christie! That is a new one.'

Further discussions followed about Beryl's pregnancy, the contradictory statements, Christie's medical knowledge, and Christie's 'straight record' since his earlier trouble with the police.

Humphreys made quick work of his closing speech. It took just 10 minutes.

Morris was caught off guard. He had thought he would be able to get all his facts together and deliver a proper closing speech in the morning. Instead, he had to sum up his defence of Evans in detail, on the spot, without having time to look at the finer points. He did the best he could, shuffling his papers, recalling details, referring to his notes and recapping the death of Geraldine. But, with no time to prepare, his effort was well short of convincing.

On that next day, then, it was the turn of Mr Justice Lewis to speak.

'Members of the jury, I have no more to say to you. You will go out now, if you will, and consider your verdict and tell me how you find, whether the accused man is guilty or not of the murder of his child, Geraldine Evans.'

After 40 minutes deliberating, the clerk of the court addressed the jury.

'Do you find the prisoner, Timothy John Evans, guilty or not guilty of the murder of Geraldine Evans?'

'Guilty.'

'You find him guilty, and that is the verdict of you all?'

'It is.'

Mr Justice Lewis, sitting directly across from Evans, asked the chilling question:

'Timothy John Evans, you stand convicted of murder. Have you anything to say why the court shall not give you judgement of death according to law?'

'No, sir.'

The judge placed the sinister-looking traditional black cap on his head and fixed his gaze on Evans.

'Timothy John Evans, the court has found you guilty of wilful murder, and the sentence of the court upon you is that you will be taken from this place to a lawful prison and thence to a place of execution and there you will suffer death by hanging, and that your body be buried within the precincts of the prison in which you shall have last been confined before your execution. And may the Lord have mercy on your soul. Amen.'

Because so few witnesses were called, the trial lasted a mere three days. Many people, including Joan Vincent, should have been called; their evidence might have explained why statements surrounding the case had been added to and changed – inconsistencies that would create problems later on. Witnesses would have made clear that the bodies of Beryl and Geraldine could not have been in the wash house during the renovation work.

Sobs were heard from the back of the court. They were coming from Christie, who knew he had helped to put the noose around the prisoner's neck. He knew that he, too, should have been implicated in some way.

He was deeply uncomfortable that Evans had accused him of murder, and even less happy when Evans's mother called him a murderer again outside the court. However, the day of the verdict, Friday 13th, was not an unlucky one for John Reginald Halliday Christie. He was free to return home.

On 15 January 1950, an appeal was made. The defence maintained that the jury had been misdirected by the judge. Christie should not have been believed, as he was not a reliable witness. He had previous convictions, including one of malicious wounding, and yet, the defence argued, the prosecution case hinged on what he had told the court.

Lord Chief Justice Goddard's view was:

'A variety of grounds have been urged by Mr Malcolm Morris, objecting to evidence and various other matters in the course of the case, but there is really only one point in this case which has any substance, or with which it is necessary to deal at any length, and that is whether or not evidence with regard to statements which this man [Evans] made with regard to the death of his wife, and an admission on his part that he had caused the death of his wife, was admissible in this case.'

Evans's police statements had sealed his fate.

The Home Secretary, James Chuter Ede, confirmed: 'The law must take its course.'

The law was due to take its course on Thursday, 9 March 1950.

Meanwhile, my own adventures were continuing unabated. I was desperate to find a way back to England, but I didn't have enough money for the voyage and needed to earn quickly.

I started working for a newspaper, going round Auckland collecting adverts. I told the guv'nor there that I needed to return to England because my sister and niece had been killed. He agreed; he just wanted to know when I was planning to leave. I stayed in the YMCA in Auckland and had my suitcase already packed. I kept it prepared just in case.

I went round the ships at Auckland docks, asking if they needed any crew. One day, chatting to the seamen, the captain of the 'Napier Star' said one of his men had jumped ship. He listened intently to my story, and how I planned to dedicate the rest of my life to the memory of Beryl and Geraldine.

Whether he could have done without me, I don't know. He said a few words, and they were music to my ears.

'We're going to be sailing tonight, so if you get down in time you can come with us.'

It took seven weeks to get back home on the Napier Star. It was a journey filled with storms and rough seas. And I worked flat out on board. It was hard work cleaning up after everyone. I scrubbed the decks and did whatever I had to do. If the crew needed their boots cleaned, I did that. If the toilets needed cleaning out, the job fell to me.

But I was just grateful to be heading home to England. We landed in Liverpool, and from there I caught a train to London, and then on to Brighton. The journey reminded me of all those times I had gone back and forth to see Beryl and Geraldine when they lived in Rillington Place.

When I arrived home to 10 Chapel Street, back in Brighton, Basil was waiting for me. He was getting a bit of a reputation as a 'Jack the Lad' and the local stud. He had worked for a green-grocer, as well as being a projectionist, but was forced to leave after 'inappropriate activities' with the owner's young daughter. He had become rather 'mouthy' and knew it all.

Basil wanted to be 'the champ of champs', as he used to call himself. He had forgotten that I had worked hard outdoors in the fresh air of New Zealand, eating good food to build me up. Although I was 17 and he was older, it seemed he still felt the need to 'put me in my place'.

I thought Basil should be in mourning for Beryl and Geraldine, rather than showing who was the tough guy in the house. When I went up to our bedroom, he followed me, ready to beat me up to show me how hard he was. He took a swing, but I ducked and gave him a right hook, smack on the jaw.

It was a terrific punch, throwing his head right back and bringing up a bruise almost straight away. He crumpled in a heap on the deck. I hung around for a bit to make sure he got up. The bruise on the side of his face grew bigger and I helped to patch him up; he was my brother, after all. I'm not sure what he told Dad – probably that he had walked into the door, or something like that. He was never going to admit that his younger brother had floored him.

And I was still fuming that he had done so little to help Beryl and Geraldine in their desperate hours of need.

Chapter 16
Timothy Evans, You Will Hang!

Albert Pierrepoint may not have known the full details about the Evans case. He made a point of not reading about trials, so that he would not form a personal opinion of guilt or innocence.

So as the hangman accepted the task of putting the rope around Evans's neck, he was probably unaware of the complex background to the case.

Pierrepoint had executed nearly 600 people during his career. In 1942, he had hanged Gordon Cummins, known as the 'Blackout Ripper', at Wandsworth Prison. Cummins murdered four women and tried to kill two others while London was in darkness during the war.

Pierrepoint had been flown to Germany to execute more than 200 Nazi war criminals including camp commandant Josef Kramer, who was known as the 'Beast of Belsen'. He also hanged camp supervisor Irma Grese, 21, who he said was the bravest prisoner he ever hanged. Later he would hang Ruth Ellis for the murder of her lover. She was the last woman to be executed in Britain.

He went to great lengths to describe his craft. 'When a man is to be executed, I and my assistant must get to the prison by four o'clock on the day before the execution, and we have to stay there until it is over. We are told the height and weight of the prisoner and are given opportunities to see him at exercise or in his cell or from some point where he cannot see us. Having got the idea of his physique, we can make the proper preparations for his execution.

'The execution chamber is usually next door to the condemned cell. It is a small room with a trap in the centre of the floor. The prisoner is escorted out of the condemned cell into the execution chamber and is placed on a white chalk mark, so that his feet are across the division of the trap. While my assistant is fastening up his legs I draw a white cap over his head and place a noose around his neck. As soon as I see that everything is ready, I pull the lever and the prisoner falls and it is all over in an instant.'

On Thursday, 9 March 1950 his assistant at Pentonville was Syd Dernley, a full-time welder and part-time executioner. Syd's hobby was collecting souvenirs from executions, including straps and white hoods. He even took the ropes away with him. In his cellar he had a working model of a set of gallows, showing visitors exactly how hangings were carried out.

Syd's claim to fame was that he was the country's fastest hangman. He talked about setting a record with Pierrepoint in the case of James Inglis, who murdered a prostitute in Hull after a row over her fees. Dernley and Pierrepoint took just seven seconds to carry out their work, from the condemned man's cell until the drop. Apparently Inglis more or less ran towards the rope, to get it over as quickly as possible.

Pierrepoint would have checked the thickness of Evans's neck. From that, he would have calculated the length of the 'drop' to ensure a speedy, humane ending. If the rope was too long, the prisoner could be decapitated. If it was too short, there was the possibility of an excruciating death from strangulation.

On the day before the hanging, the two executioners studied Evans in the exercise yard as Pierrepoint described. They had to assess his fitness, his mood, and how he would react when the time came. He had been weighed at 137lbs, and a sandbag of that weight had been placed on the rope to stretch it. Normally, if any stretch was detected, the length of the drop would be adjusted accordingly.

Dernley thought Evans had a 'diminutive size' and that he looked frail and careworn the evening before the hanging. He and Pierrepoint had looked through the peephole in the condemned man's cell door. They were again checking on his general physical condition, still assessing his mood and any other characteristics they might pick up on. He could put up a bit of a struggle, for all they knew.

Dernley said that early the next morning, Pierrepoint seemed to be on edge, snapping at him as the final preparations were made. Syd said he went into the condemned man's cell, and Evans turned round and looked at him with the most terrified eyes he had ever seen.

With the white hood placed over his head, and all preparations complete just before 9am, Evans took his final breaths. We will never know whether he actually said anything. Some reports suggest that Evans said: 'Christie done it, Christie done it.' Other records say that he did not utter a word.

Pierrepoint stepped forward to pull the lever.

It was all over.

It had taken just 15 seconds from the moment Evans left the condemned cell until he fell through the trap door, with hood and noose firmly in place.

Timothy Evans was buried in the cemetery at Pentonville. There was little ceremony, with not much attention paid at all to the burial.

Pierrepoint said he thought Evans 'an insignificant little man.' Although not normally concerned with the events surrounding a case, he later said he was 'absolutely certain' that Evans was guilty.

At home, things were difficult. Beryl and Geraldine stayed on my mind, day after day. Dad was drinking and smoking heavily.

Basil was being a general nuisance. Pat had become involved with the Jehovah's Witnesses, knocking at doors all the time. And Marguerita was insufferable.

I needed to get out, so I joined the army. I thought it would be a quick way of getting my head right, escaping from Brighton for a bit and planning the rest of my life. Basil wanted to join up too, but he stuttered, so they wouldn't let him in: if he were to be promoted, he wouldn't be able to give an order. It upset Basil that I was accepted and he wasn't allowed to join up.

I served in Cyprus and Egypt, returning fit and fresh to get to the bottom of what had really happened at 10 Rillington Place.

I found out that the case was baffling, riddled with contradictions, lies and deceit.

It was that way from start to finish.

Chapter 17
The Serial Killer

Timothy Evans was hanged for the murder of my niece, Geraldine, but the story of 10 Rillington Place was far from over.

I was unhappy with the law, for charging him with Beryl's murder but not convicting him of the crime. They had only needed the one conviction to hang Timothy Evans, so he never faced trial for Beryl's murder. I felt a deep inner anger that Evans had not been punished for both killings.

Little did I know that the one man I thought I could trust at 10 Rillington Place would soon face grim charges of his own.

I had played with Reg Christie's friendly mongrel Judy in his back garden so many times, totally unaware that there was anything peculiar about him. All those times I had tea and sticky buns with 'Uncle Reg', he played cards with me and looked after me as if it were the most normal thing in the world.

Two years on from Evans's execution, in 1952, Reg Christie abruptly moved out of Rillington Place, with no explanation.

A West Indian couple, Beresford Dubois Brown and Lena Stewart, were living in the top-floor flat at Rillington Place where Beryl had once stayed. Beresford was a jazz musician who arrived in Plymouth from Kingston, Jamaica, aboard the Colombie, a French passenger ship, in December 1950.

With the Christie flat empty, Beresford wanted to take advantage of the extra space and make use of the kitchen downstairs. The landlord couldn't see any reason why not and, just to be helpful, Beresford thought he would tidy the place up a bit. There were various assorted items of rubbish scattered around the ground-floor flat, including some unidentified clothes, which he bagged up and took out into the yard, thinking no more of it.

On 24 March, Beresford was feeling quite pleased about his clean-up and thought, while he was using the kitchen, that he might as well have some entertainment and listen to some jazz. He owned a wireless set, and he reckoned it would sit neatly on the wall. The only thing was, it needed to be supported by brackets.

He looked around the room for a suitable place to put it, and found the perfect spot: the entrance to the alcove.

Beresford knocked at the wall to find a good place to drill holes for the brackets. The alcove had a wooden door, and wallpaper had been pasted over it.

Beresford couldn't understand why wallpaper had been applied to cover the door. Christie had seemingly papered over the entrance for no apparent reason, covering the alcove with the thinnest of materials.

Puzzled, Beresford peeled back the top corner of the wallpaper and shone his torch inside.

He got the shock of his life.

There was a naked body in a sitting position inside the alcove.

Beresford rushed upstairs to fetch another tenant, Mr Williams, who also had a look into the alcove. Both men were stunned.

Beresford ran to the same phone box where Beryl had once called the police after her horrendous treatment by Timothy Evans. The police were soon there in force, combing the property and attracting the attention of the entire area.

Pathologist Dr Francis Camps was quickly on the scene and identified not just one, but three bodies in the alcove.

'One was on its back with the legs vertical against the back of the cupboard,' he later stated. 'It was wrapped in a blanket, tied round the ankles with a piece of wire, and the torso covered with earth and ashes.

'Another body, also wrapped in a blanket and tied round the ankles with a sock, was lying on top of the other in a similar position and also covered with earth and ashes.

'The third body was sitting in an upright position and kept in that position by her brassiere, to the back of which was tied the end of the blanket from the feet of the middle body.

'Later that night I examined the front room on the ground floor and noticed some loose boards in the middle of the room. I lifted the boards and, completely buried in earth and rubble, was another body wrapped in a blanket.'

The fourth body was none other than Ethel Christie, Reg's wife, who I had last seen serving us afternoon tea.

All four bodies were taken to Kensington Mortuary by the police for further examination.

The police scoured the entire house, before conducting a thorough search of the garden. There, they uncovered the remains of two more bodies. They were all women.

To this day, I still think about running around in the garden with Christie's dog, totally oblivious to the fact that bodies were lying underneath my feet.

* * *

The man I had known as 'Uncle Reg', who appeared kindly and good-natured, had spent years preying on prostitutes and vulnerable young women.

Reg Christie cashed in on the general confusion surrounding missing people during and after the war. He knew that a woman could be reported missing and presumed a victim of the bombing, when in reality she was under his control in 10 Rillington Place.

Ruth Fuerst was the first of Christie's victims. She was an Austrian refugee aged 21. Born Ruth Margarete Christine Fuerst on 2 August 1922 in Bad Vöslau, Lower Austria, she was half Jewish, and lost contact with her parents after the Germans marched into her country in 1938. She arrived in Britain in June 1939, months before the outbreak of war, and found some casual work, but was interned as an alien on the Isle of Wight, where she stayed until December 1940.

After her release, she headed to London and found work as a waitress at the Mayfair Hotel. While she was there she had a baby by a Cypriot man. There was no way Ruth could afford to look after the child, and so the baby was adopted.

Ruth continued working as a waitress, living in Elgin Crescent, before moving the short distance to Oxford Gardens in Notting Hill.

Christie would have come across her either as a local resident, or in his role as a War Reserve Constable, because her home was about 300 yards from Rillington Place.

With the war effort ramping up, Ruth found a job as a munitions worker. It is believed that she topped up her earnings by working as a part-time prostitute, although we can't be certain of that.

At any rate, Christie came across Ruth and invited her back to 10 Rillington Place. During one visit, while Ethel was away seeing her sister in Sheffield, Christie's twisted urges got the better of him. While they were having intercourse, he produced a rope and strangled Ruth.

Initially, the body was hidden under the floorboards in the front room, but Christie soon moved her into the wash house and eventually, when no one was looking, buried her in the garden.

Christie was excited at how easy it had been to satisfy his perverted urges, murder Ruth and conceal her body. He began the hunt for another victim.

Muriel Amelia Eady was born at 20 Baron Road, Plaistow, West Ham, on 14 October 1912. She was the youngest of four children and her parents were William Eady and Fanny Louisa Hooper.

In September 1939, Muriel lived in Cambridge, working as a laundry and domestic servant. She moved to Putney, southwest London, in 1940 and lived with her aunt Martha in Roskell Road. She worked for a company in Chiswick making aircraft parts, then found a job on the assembly line at Ultra Electric Limited in Acton, putting radios together.

Unfortunately for Muriel, one of the clerks at Ultra was John Reginald Halliday Christie. He was eager to claim his second victim.

Muriel suffered from bronchitis, and Christie said he had a special cure for her condition. She visited 10 Rillington Place, but the first time she brought a friend, Ernest Lawson. However, after discussing his potential cure, Muriel was invited back on her own.

On Saturday, 7 October 1944, she had lunch with her aunt and then went off to meet Christie. In the meantime, Christie had prepared a concoction to help Muriel with her bronchitis. Muriel Eady arrived alone at Rillington Place, tapped on the rusty knocker, and waited for the door to be answered.

As usual, Christie opened the door, had a quick look around, and took Muriel's coat. In she went, keen to have her symptoms relieved with a magic cure.

She sat in Christie's rope chair, where I would often sit in years to come, while he stirred some Friar's Balsam and water in a jar. The jar had a tube coming out, connected to a mouthpiece, which Christie asked her to put on. Muriel would have detected the strong aromas pouring out to clear her sinuses.

What she did not know was that Christie had connected a second tube to the gas supply near the rope chair. Muriel soon fell unconscious.

Christie strangled Muriel Eady with a stocking. His depraved urges knew no restraint any more. He raped her dead body, before carrying her into the wash house. When the coast was clear, he dug another shallow grave next to that of Ruth Fuerst, and buried Muriel's body.

Muriel's aunt, Mrs Hooper, was concerned because her niece had told her, 'Shan't be late.' Muriel had been smartly dressed in a black frock and camel coat when she went out.

Where had she gone? The Second World War was still raging, so she had reason enough to be concerned.

On the Monday her employers assumed that she was ill. With no news by 25 October, they asked for a medical certificate. Christie himself had taken sick leave from 2 to 10 October, carefully covering up his meeting with Muriel on 7 October.

Muriel's cousin, Wilfrid Dunn, reported her missing at Putney Police Station. The family assumed tragedy had struck, as a nearby dance hall in Putney had been bombed.

Christie had got away with murder for a second time.

What follows in the history of Reg Christie is a long gap until 1949, when he was involved in the aftermath of the murders of Beryl and Geraldine. Even Christie himself later said he was unsure whether he had committed more murders during that period.

The next definite victim was closer to home.

Ethel Christie was friendly and capable around the house. I knew about Uncle Reg's health problems, but Ethel never mentioned any issues of her own. However, she made frequent visits to Dr Odess from 1948 onwards, for a variety of complaints including her frayed nerves. I suppose the trials and tribulations of living in 10 Rillington Place took their toll.

The doctor gave Ethel a sedative to take during the day and sleeping tablets, too. Ethel was also worried about her varicose veins, a skin condition and rheumatism. The doctor did what he could by prescribing ointment. Her last appointment with Dr Odess was on 28 August 1952, when she had only months to live.

The Christies' sex life had become virtually non-existent. It just 'fell away', Christie said. They never talked about stopping that part of the relationship; Christie maintained he always had a strong affection for his wife despite the lack of physical contact.

In the wake of the Evans trial, Christie was fully aware that Ethel knew too much and suspected even more. Apart from his involvement in my sister's case, he continually spied on young women and always enjoyed the company of prostitutes. Perhaps he thought Ethel would eventually go the police. She wasn't well enough to keep up her trips to see her family in Sheffield, as she suffered from chronic arthritis and rheumatism.

Her days at Rillington Place were numbered.

The year was 1952. From Friday, 5 December to Tuesday, 9 December, the 'Great Smog of London' covered the city. It was difficult just to breathe.

Christie was working as an invoice clerk with British Road Services, where he had been employed since June 1950. He had started at the Shepherd's Bush depot and later moved to the one at Hampstead. He left because he said he had a better job to go to in Sheffield – which of course was not true. He was gripped by the need to plan further crimes.

The weather was very cold, there was no wind, and the whole of London choked during that awful smog. A thick layer formed over the entire city, killing 4,000 people and up to 6,000 more in the following months. Factories continued to belch out smoke, everybody burned coal, and when a fog came along you couldn't see your hand in front of your face. I thought again of my mother breathing in all that muck a few years earlier, worsening her condition.

On Friday, 12 December, Ethel handed in her laundry to Maxwell Laundries in Walmer Road. She took along a quilt, two pillow cases and a sheet, receiving a receipt on the premises. She also returned a book, one of the *Penny Poets* collection, to North Kensington Library. She didn't take out another book to read.

The following day, Saturday, she went next door to watch television with Mrs Swan. It was an almost daily routine for the women.

The laundry was never collected, and that was the last time Ethel and Mrs Swan would ever sit together.

Just after eight o'clock on 14 December, she was lying in her silk nightdress, thinking about the day ahead. Suddenly her husband grabbed a stocking and pulled it around her neck.

Christie held the stocking tightly until his wife stopped struggling.

Ethel Christie was dead. Reg Christie wrapped her body in a blanket, secured it with a safety pin, and deposited her under the floorboards of the front room. He threw some rubble on top of her and put the floor back together again.

What would Christie tell neighbours to explain the sudden disappearance of his wife? It was simple enough: he said Ethel had gone back to her family in Sheffield.

A more difficult question was how he would explain his wife's disappearance to her family. She had made regular visits to Sheffield, and he knew that questions would be asked and time would run out for him at some stage.

Christie found an unsent letter that Ethel had written to her sister in Sheffield, dated 10 December, four days before she died. He changed the date to 15 December, adding a note to say they had had no envelopes and so the letter was sent from his workplace. Christie had given up his job by then, but he must have gone in to post the letter, making everything look authentic.

In truth, Ethel was already dead when that letter was finally sent.

Subsequent letters from Christie claimed that Ethel was too ill to write, because of the rheumatism in her hands.

And so he kept composing letters, purporting to be from both of them, and even included gifts. At Christmas, he kept up the pretence with this short note to Ethel's sister, Lily:

DON'T WORRY SHE IS OK. I SHALL COOK XMAS DINNER. REG

Ethel has got me to write her cards for her as her rheumatism in her fingers is not so good just now. Doctor says it's the weather and she will be OK in 2 or 3 days. I am rubbing them for her and it makes them easier. We are in good health now and as soon as Ethel can write (perhaps by Saturday) she is going to send a letter. Hope you like the present. She selected it for you.

Reg

On 16 December, Reg Christie sold his wife's wedding ring in a jewellery shop. A few days later, he sold her watch as well.

As Reg and Ethel disliked living with the West Indian community in Notting Hill, Lily was worried about the couple in their surroundings. She wrote to Ethel expressing concerns, saying she would have been happier for Ethel to come and live in Sheffield, but Reg failed to reply.

It was getting more and more difficult to keep up the pretence. He told made-up stories to neighbours Mrs Swan and Mrs Grimes, even holding up a fake telegram from his wife and saying she was still with her sister in Sheffield.

Naturally, unpleasant odours began to seep from the floorboards, with fellow tenants and neighbours wondering what was going on.

Lena Stewart and Beresford Brown had moved into Beryl's former flat upstairs. Lena, who stayed home looking after her and Brown's baby, encountered Christie most days, and noticed that Christie was going around splashing disinfectant inside and outside 10 Rillington Place. She could see that he was splashing what appeared to be Jeyes Fluid in the passage from the front door, and the scent was very strong.

'He disinfected the back yard,' she said later. 'I saw him pouring it down the drains. I also saw him put it outside under the window of his front room where I used to put my pram. He told me one morning that somebody had thrown dirty water down the drain. He never spoke to me about why he disinfected the front passage or outside the front room window. He generally did the disinfecting between 8.30am and 9am when everybody had left the house to go to work.'

Mr Hookway, the furniture dealer, was back at Rillington Place on 8 January 1953. Christie was planning to escape and move elsewhere, and he needed money. Mr Hookway took away items including a couple of sideboards, a chest of drawers, linoleum and some chairs. He left behind the mattress, as it was in poor condition. He didn't like the look of the rope chair either, and declined to take it.

Whereas the Evans furnishings in 1949 had been new and fetched £40, Christie had to accept £12. Mr Hookway thought the flat looked as if the Devil himself had been living there, with the surroundings in such a state. I remember the place being quite neat and tidy when Ethel was still around. But by now, Christie was concentrating more on his murders than carrying on with the housework.

When Mr Hookway visited, Christie was arguing with the landlord, Charles Brown, possibly over the rent, though it could also have been because of the new tenants occupying the rooms on the first and second floors. Christie hated living in the same building as the recent inhabitants; it was well known that he had asked local politicians to keep foreigners out of the area.

Charles Brown was the landlord of 10 Rillington Place from 1950. He lived in nearby Silchester Terrace. There were many complaints about the running of the house: at one stage 10 Rillington Place was an out-of-hours illegal drinking club. Charles Brown was a doorman at a legal club in Soho, and apparently guided revellers round to Rillington Place for more entertainment after closing time. There were reports of drug-dealing in the press, and so the area certainly took a turn for the worse.

At any rate, Mr Brown stopped receiving rent from Christie during the first week of January 1953. As he had given up his job, he needed more money to live on. He was well practised at copying Ethel's handwriting, with the letters to her sister, so he decided to try his hand at fraud. Ethel had opened an account with Yorkshire Penny Bank in 1944, and he had the idea of trying to collect her savings.

Reg Christie wrote to the Haymarket branch of the society, forging Ethel's signature and asking for the account to be closed. The manager compared the signature with a previous one, and it seemed to match. There was £10 15s 2d in the account, and the amount was forwarded to Christie. Another cheque, this time for £8, arrived after he sold his wife's clothes. He managed to claim some benefits as well.

Christie was ready to strike again. With Ethel out of the way, he could pick and choose his victims. He was stalking cafes, seeking out the vulnerable and offering help to them.

His next victim was Rita Nelson, a 25-year-old unfortunate who dabbled in prostitution. She was born on 16 October 1927 at the City Hospital in Belfast to a highly religious Protestant family. Her father was described as a labourer and her mother a housewife – it was not a well-to-do family. She was able to put on a posh accent, though, to disguise her humble beginnings.

Rita had built up a criminal record in her early years. She appeared in court in Belfast for theft, assault, prostitution and being drunk and disorderly. She was only 13 when she faced the first charge of theft. I don't know how she managed to pay the fines, because the drunk and disorderly case alone cost her 40 shillings. She even served a short jail sentence.

She had been attacked during her teens and her assailant tried to strangle her. She survived, with a fractured bone in her neck. No one was ever arrested for that brutal attack.

By all accounts, she wasn't really a criminal – just totally lost and confused in her impoverished surroundings, and looking for a way out. Rita hoped that way out lay in England, where perhaps she could get regular work and go straight. Along with her cousin, James Boyd, she caught the ferry from Belfast to Heysham in Lancashire.

On that ferry, people would have noticed that Rita was a striking woman. She was slim, about 5ft 5in, with wiry brown hair, brown eyes and bright red nails and lips. She didn't smile much because she was missing several teeth.

Rita and James visited her sister Mae at 80 Ladbroke Grove, a few hundred yards from Rillington Place. James found work as a carpenter in the Stratford area of East London, while Rita got a job as a waitress. She tried hard to stay out of trouble and managed to avoid any more arrests.

However, Rita failed to find work that suited her. For one reason or another, her jobs as kitchen maid, waitress or hospital orderly lasted just a few weeks.

Shortly before Christmas 1952, Rita visited her sister in Ladbroke Grove. For whatever reason, she didn't stay there, and instead rented a room locally, while her cousin returned to Belfast. On 18 January 1953, Rita's mother Lily received a letter saying that her daughter was doing fine. And she was six months pregnant. Rita's plan was to return to Belfast the following month and prepare to have the baby.

She managed to hide the fact that she was pregnant from her latest employer, a tearoom in Shepherd's Bush. They eventually found out, and tried to help Rita by locating a home for unmarried mothers. Oddly, Rita turned down her employer's offers of assistance.

The last sighting of Rita was on Friday, 16 January 1953, when she went to post a letter to her mother. The next day, her landlady knocked at her door because the rent was overdue. The landlady sensed that something was wrong, and reported Rita missing.

Christie and Rita met in a cafe at Notting Hill Gate, either on the Friday or the day after. He lured her back to 10 Rillington Place, probably with the promise of helping to improve her lot. Maybe he offered her money as an inducement to come home with him.

The decision to go there cost Rita her life.

She sat in the infamous rope chair I had played cards in so many times, and he gassed and strangled her. It is not clear exactly how he administered the gas. It is believed that Rita put up some sort of a struggle, and she may well have tried to batter him with a frying pan.

But Christie overpowered her. He raped Rita, no doubt when she was already unconscious or dead, and wrapped her body in a blanket. He tied plastic flex around her ankles and hid her in the alcove. He took off her knickers and replaced them with a couple of his vests, like a nappy. Tragically, her baby's life ebbed away too.

The next month, Christie seized the opportunity to kill again. This time his victim was Kathleen Maloney, 26, a prostitute who hailed originally from Plymouth. Her hair was dyed a dirty blonde colour, she was about 5ft 2in, her face was on the plump side and she had brown eyes.

Kathleen was born in King Street, Plymouth, on 19 August 1926. Her father was a rag-and-bone man and she had two sisters. Her parents died in the late 1920s and she was looked after by an aunt before going to a Catholic home. After a spell at a convent in Plymouth, where she was accused of stealing a coat, she was sent to another convent in Southampton. She was said to be out of control and returned to Plymouth in 1943.

Kathleen ran away to London and plied her trade with American servicemen in the latter stages of the war. She was placed on probation after appearing at Bow Street Magistrates' Court charged with being a vagrant. A jail term followed for breaking the conditions of her probation.

Back to Southampton she went with another prostitute, and another two jail sentences followed. Her offences included prostitution, being drunk and disorderly, using foul language and assaulting a police officer. She was also described as 'likely to cause infection'. More jail time followed as she travelled between Southampton, Reading and Liverpool.

She went on to have five children between 1946 and 1950; four went to a children's home and the other was adopted.

Kathleen saw Christie as some sort of salvation. She was sleeping in public toilets in Edgware Road after being released from Holloway Prison. I am sure that, at some stage, Kathleen would have come across Christie in a cafe as he scoured the area for potential victims.

A friend of Kathleen's, Maureen Briggs, has recounted how they met Christie in a pub. Maureen agreed that Christie could take pictures of her in the nude, which he did in a small room off Marylebone Road. Christie persuaded Kathleen to take pictures of him and Maureen in the nude. They felt uneasy about the whole operation. He gave them £1 each for their troubles.

Early in February – it is difficult to establish an exact date – the women spotted Christie in a different pub. He bought them drinks. One of the people in the pub said later that Kathleen had nowhere to sleep, but a man she met would help her – presumably Christie. They left the pub together; Kathleen was completely drunk.

Again, his victim sat in the rope chair and the gas was administered. She fought back, but to no avail. It's probable that he strangled her during sex. He forced himself on her, either then or after she was dead. When his grisly task was completed, he shoved Rita's body into the alcove, again with an improvised nappy.

Around this time, Christie wondered what to do about Judy the dog. She was now 14 years old, and there was little money to look after her. She had been healthy and full of life when I ran around the garden with her while Ethel was still alive.

Judy had an eye infection at the age of 14. It didn't seem too serious, but there was an animal first aid man called Ernest Jacobs living nearby in Clarendon Road, and Christie paid him five shillings to put Judy down. It was yet another measure of his cruelty – she was a lovely dog and had stayed loyal to Reg and Ethel for 12 years.

There had also been a tabby cat that ran around the Christies' garden back in the days when I visited. I was never sure whether it belonged to the Christies or another neighbouring family, but apparently the animal was likewise put down by the RSPCA.

Next on Christie's list was Hectorina Maclennan. Hectorina was 26 years old, a morally upstanding woman who just wanted to pay her way and have an ordinary home and family without causing trouble.

However, trouble, in the shape of Reg Christie, came looking for her.

Hectorina was born on 18 February 1926 in Grovepark Street, a rundown part of Glasgow. She had three brothers and two sisters. It was a close-knit family, struggling to survive in times of poverty. The family had nothing.

Hectorina, known as Ina, was about 5ft 4in, with a young-looking face. She was slightly cross-eyed. She was not a typical target for Christie, with no record of sex work or criminality; she had actually enjoyed good times in her life.

Her father, William, had first come to London in 1944, and the family followed four years later. She became involved with Khin Muang Sou Hla, who served with the Burmese Air Force. She spent some time living with him at his base in Hampshire, and by all accounts was happy with her lot.

He was then posted to Wales. She decided to live with her parents and eight-year-old daughter in Earl's Court, just over two miles from Rillington Place.

She worked at an usherette at the Imperial Cinema in Portobello Road. All the time she seemed to be getting closer to Reg Christie.

Ina married Khin on 12 October 1950 while she was pregnant with her second child. Unfortunately, their relationship ran into problems and Khin returned to Burma. In October 1952, Ina's family returned to Scotland and she decided to stay with her two children in London. Her fate was sealed.

Ina became highly vulnerable. She met an ex-convict, Alex Baker, who was married with five children; Ina babysat for one of them. His wife Dorothy found out that they were having an affair, and told Alex to leave. Alex and Ina moved into a furnished flat near Ladbroke Grove, but they argued a lot, and Alex went back to his wife.

Ina couldn't afford the rent, so she started sleeping rough in doorways. She looked terrible and unkempt, wearing ragged clothes. Some have claimed that she was a prostitute, but there is no clear evidence of this. There was a National Assistance Board at the time, and she received some help, but scraping by each day was becoming impossible for Ina.

She encountered Christie in a cafe, and no doubt he offered to be of assistance. In the meantime, she had also teamed up again with Alex, who had left his wife once more. To make matters worse, Ina was pregnant.

On 3 March 1953, in the evening, Ina kept an appointment with Christie outside Ladbroke Grove Tube station. Unfortunately for her stalker, Alex appeared there as well.

They all went back to Rillington Place. It was obvious that the couple couldn't afford any rent and, after some toing and froing, Christie said they could stay for a few nights. Still, he had to get rid of Alex somehow in order to be alone with Hectorina.

His chance came soon enough. In the morning, Alex and Ina left to go to the National Assistance Board in Shepherd's Bush. Christie must have persuaded Ina to see him at Rillington Place around midday.

Alex was expecting to meet her in a cafe later that afternoon. He had no idea that she had agreed to meet Christie.

We can't be sure what happened when Ina got to Rillington Place. She certainly would have sat in the rope chair. Perhaps they discussed her pregnancy, but there was no evidence later of an attempted abortion.

It appears that Reg Christie gassed Hectorina, strangled her with a length of rope and raped her. I believe that she fought back hard, but Christie had the element of surprise during what must have been a ferocious attack. Soon, after he had had his way with her, she was thrust into the alcove alongside Rita and Kathleen.

Alex Baker, waiting to meet her that afternoon, was more than confused. He called Hectorina his wife, although she wasn't, and had become extremely close to her. There was no way she would miss a meeting with him and simply disappear. It was totally out of character. He decided to pay a visit to 10 Rillington Place.

Christie opened the various doors in his flat to show that no one else was there – a curious thing to do – and then he put the kettle on. It is extraordinary to imagine Baker sitting there, having a brew with Ina's murderer. Ina's body was only a few feet away in the alcove, no doubt still warm, in a sitting position, with her bra secured to the blanket around Kathleen Maloney. There was a nasty smell, Baker recalled later, that no doubt came from Christie's earlier victims, placed in the alcove.

Baker was still confused by Hectorina's disappearance, and told Christie he was going off to look for her; the usual haunts around Shepherd's Bush would be a good start. Christie thought it would be a good idea to join the search, and so he set off with Baker on the hunt for the anxious visitor's 'wife'. The search was abandoned at around 9pm.

That wasn't the end of Christie's attentions. He kept in touch with Baker, enquiring about Hectorina, and making sure his concerns were appreciated. He even went to the Labour Exchange, found Baker and said he was continuing to look out for Hectorina. Baker also visited Rillington Place, to check if there were any updates. The door wasn't answered.

Christie was actively looking for other vulnerable targets. One was Mary O'Neill, originally from Ireland, who had been involved in prostitution. She also had a three-week old baby. Christie and Mary met by chance at Ladbroke Grove railway station, where the friendly stranger offered to help her. He guided her to the National Assistance office in Hammersmith and provided her with money, tea and cigarettes.

Mary visited 10 Rillington Place on a few occasions, where she heard stories about the First World War, the police commendations and the sad, natural death of Ethel. I imagine she sat in the rope chair, like Christie's other victims. He tried to kiss her once and she screamed – so that approach failed.

When Mary visited Rillington Place, she had told her boyfriend where she was going. The knowledge of that prevented Christie from doing anything incriminating. Mary's caution and foresight saved her life.

Helen Sunderland, who met Christie in Piccadilly, also had a fortunate escape from his clutches. As usual, cigarettes and tea were offered as Christie tried to strike up a friendship. Back they went to Rillington Place in a taxi, as Christie's head filled with evil thoughts.

He asked Helen to take her clothes off and, when she refused, Christie appeared with a dark rug. She reached forward to look under the rug, and was terrified to discover that Christie was holding a cord several feet long. His intentions were clear.

She banged on a door as he approached, holding both ends of the cord, and then kicked him. Christie's glasses fell off, and as he scrambled round on the floor trying to find them, she managed to open a window, climb out and run off along the street. She must have had a good reason for not getting the police round straight away.

With two failed attempts now on his conscience, Christie realised that time was running out. With no job, little furniture and several bodies in or around the premises, he was in a fix. The only solution, he thought, was to sub-let his flat on the ground floor. He had no right to do so, but in the situation he had created for himself, it was his only option.

He came across a Mrs Reilly in Ladbroke Grove, looking in a window advertising flats to let.

'I might be able to help you,' he whispered. 'Have you found what you're looking for? If not, I could have the answer.'

Mrs Reilly had no reason to doubt that he was genuine. He told her that he had new job prospects in Birmingham and his wife had already gone ahead. He most likely wouldn't have mentioned the address, 10 Rillington Place, because of all the previous publicity around the Evans case. Perhaps he hoped it had faded from her memory.

'Why don't you come back and look at the flat?'

Back they went – it was only a short walk – and Mrs Reilly could see that the accommodation was spartan, but adequate. Later her husband came along too, and they decided to go ahead and rent. They paid three months in advance, amounting to £7 13s 7d. They also gave him £1 for some extras he left behind. Christie even provided them with a receipt.

And so, on 20 March 1953, the Reillys moved in and Christie moved out. However, he was a long way behind with the rent, had no right to sub-let the property, and six bodies were waiting to be discovered in 10 Rillington Place. For the Reillys, it was hardly going to be 'home sweet home'.

Off Reg Christie went with a suitcase borrowed from the Reillys. As well as his own possessions, he included some of Kathleen Maloney's clothing. He left behind the clothes of his other victims; perhaps Kathleen was his favourite and he wanted to take away a 'trophy'.

Dr Odess was one of the last people to see him in the Notting Hill area. The doctor asked how his patient was feeling. Christie said he certainly felt better, with some attacks of pain, but he made no further appointments.

Mrs Reilly noticed a strange smell in the kitchen. She wondered what on earth it could be.

Later, she recalled: 'I thought it was the dog, as he used to have a dog there. It was a noticeable smell.'

The landlord Charles Brown dropped in to Rillington Place later that day, expecting to see Christie and hoping to receive the rent arrears. Instead of 'Uncle Reg' answering the door, it was a couple he had never seen before.

'Who are you? What are you doing here?'

'We've moved in. Mr Christie took our rent money and we're living here now.'

Fortunately for her, Mr Brown was sympathetic and allowed them to stay the night, although he insisted they had to leave in the morning. The Reillys had been conned, and had to start again from scratch, losing their hard-earned cash. £7 was a lot of money at the time. Mr Brown made some enquiries along the street, but no one knew anything of Christie's whereabouts.

Shortly afterwards, purely by chance, Beresford Brown stumbled across the source of that terrible smell.

* * *

Crowds gathered outside 10 Rillington Place as the police went about their business. Among the gruesome items they found in the house was a tobacco tin containing pubic hairs.

'Uncle Reg' was a wanted man. His picture could be seen on the front pages of all the newspapers, with questions circling as to whether he would strike again. People were being urged to look out for him.

Police gave newspapers a full description: they said he was 55 years old, 5ft 9in, of slim build, with dark hair, thin on top, and clean shaven. The wanted man had a sallow complexion, with a long nose, and was wearing horn-rimmed spectacles. He had top and bottom dentures. When last seen, he was wearing a dark blue herring-bone suit under a fawn raincoat with a belt. He also wore a brown trilby hat. They said he walked 'with a military bearing', so that people would notice his purposeful stride.

There were reported sightings of him in Trowbridge in Wiltshire and Bognor Regis in Sussex, as well as other far-flung parts of the country. But all the while, he was skulking around London, trying to keep a low profile despite his distinctive appearance. Even football fans were looking out for him in the crowd at matches.

He just wandered around, frequenting cafes. He booked into Rowton House in King's Cross Road for seven nights. This was a former workhouse that had catered for evacuees during the war, as they prepared to go to their countryside locations. Refugees from Belgium and Poland also stayed there. In the 1950s the building catered for people registered with the National Assistance Board, and so Christie was eligible to stay. As soon as newspapers announced the nationwide search for him, he went back onto the streets and continued to walk around aimlessly.

It has been reported that he met a lady called Margaret Wilson in a cafe and started chatting to her. Apparently she told Christie she was pregnant, and that no doubt inflamed his old debauched desires. However, he had nowhere to go to satisfy those cravings, and he had to say farewell to Margaret without offering any medical assistance.

Cold, hungry, and wearing wet clothes, he really had had enough. On 31 March, just after 9am, he was spotted on the embankment near Putney Bridge by PC Thomas Ledger, who took him for 'a down-and-out'. PC Ledger could see he was unkempt, and no doubt hungry, so he asked him what he was doing there. The policeman wondered if he was trying to find work. Christie answered that he was looking for work, but needed some paperwork to come through. The policeman asked him for his name and address.

'John Waddington, 35 Westbourne Grove.'

'Do you have anything to prove your identity?'

He said he had nothing.

PC Ledger asked Christie to remove his hat, and the game was up. That familiar dome-shaped head appeared on top of the circular glasses. PC Ledger 'recognised him quite easily'.

Christie was apprehended and taken straight to Putney police station.

At the station, officers could see he was exhausted and hungry. He was given some food – the first time he had eaten in four days. He was told he was going to be taken to Notting Hill police station, where he would be charged with the murder of his wife.

Chief Inspector Albert Griffin informed Christie that Ethel's body had been found under the floorboards in the front room. Did he have anything to say?

Christie cried and confessed, although he said it was a mercy killing, as his wife had been so unwell. He also admitted to killing

Kathleen Maloney, Rita Nelson and Hectorina Maclennan, maintaining that he acted in self-defence. He was being threatened by them and had no choice but to fight back, he claimed.

A body search revealed a newspaper cutting of the Evans case, his rent book, marriage certificate, St John Ambulance card, National Insurance documents, union card, ration book and identity card. There were also a few coins. He seemed to be giving money away, although he had so little. At Rowton House he paid almost twice as much as was needed for his breakfast and told them to keep the change.

Soon he would be on trial for his life. Like Evans, he faced the prospect of an appointment with executioner Albert Pierrepoint. The only thing that could save him might be a plea of insanity. The court proceedings were still to come.

For now, John Reginald Halliday Christie was under arrest. And people were jubilant that he was off the streets for good. As with Evans, he would face a single murder charge, as that was still the system at the time. He was charged with the murder of his wife, Ethel.

Christie was held in Brixton Prison, where he played chess with prisoners and was generally well behaved. He praised the prison officers for making his life as bearable as possible, though he wrote down that he was 'somewhat fuddled and dazed'.

Included in the list of visiting medical experts was Dr John Matheson, who had also seen Timothy Evans in Brixton in 1950.

The doctor shared one thing in common with Christie: they had both served during the First World War. Dr Matheson, who had also had experience at HMP Holloway, had lost his left leg and the sight in his right eye.

Dr Matheson found that Christie was sane and fit to plead in court. He confirmed Christie's high level of intelligence, with an IQ of 128. Christie did show signs of emotion, and wept as they talked about the death of his wife, Ethel. The doctor didn't detect the presence of delusions or hallucinations.

Christie's statements to police showed him trying again to make it look like a mercy killing. Here is one of his stories:

'My wife had been suffering a great deal from persecution and assaults from people in the house No. 10 Rillington Place, and had to undergo treatment at the doctor for her nerves. In December she was becoming very frightened and was afraid to go about the house when they were about, and she got very depressed. On 14 December, I was awakened at about 8.15am. I think it was by my wife moving about in bed. I sat up and saw that she appeared to be convulsive, her face was blue and she was choking. I did what I could to try and restore her breathing but it was hopeless. It appeared too late to call for assistance. That's when I couldn't bear to see her, so I got a stocking and tied it round her neck to put her to sleep.

'Then I got out of bed and saw a small bottle and a cup half full of water on a small table near the bed. I noticed that the bottle contained two phenol barbitone tablets and it originally contained 25. I knew then that she must have taken the remainder. I got them from the hospital because I couldn't sleep.'

Those drugs were not found in Ethel's body during the post-mortem examination.

Christie said he left her on the bed for two or three days, wondering what to do. He recalled that there were some loose floorboards in the front room, so he moved some of the furniture and rolled back the linoleum. He placed Ethel's body in a blanket and dragged her into the space in the floor, then covered the body with earth. After that, he replaced the floorboards.

An appointment with executioner Pierrepoint seemed imminent.

Chapter 18
The Lies of Uncle Reg

Three years on from Beryl's death, Christie was now about to go on trial for the murder of Ethel. He looked a guilty man.

The defence considered their options, but Christie's chances seemed slim. The only plausible way out was a plea of insanity, in order to avoid the death penalty.

On 8 June 1953, Christie made a shocking statement that would cast an even longer shadow over the gruesome history of 10 Rillington Place. He had decided that, to prove his insanity, his best strategy was to claim he had killed as many people as possible. 'The more the madder' was the phrase used in such cases at the time, and this, he hoped, would alleviate his guilt in the eyes of the court, and lead to a lesser sentence.

Purely to aid his claim of insanity, Christie decided to add my beloved sister to his list of purported victims. He asserted that it was not Timothy Evans, but he himself who had killed Beryl.

This cruel, gratuitous new allegation came as a hammer blow to me and my family.

His tall tale began with the aftermath of Evans's affair with Lucy Endicott:

'Evans went out with the blonde [Lucy] and he was carrying a suitcase. He came back alone later. The next day, Mrs Evans told my wife that she was going down to the police court to get a separation from her husband. My wife and I had a chat and we agreed between us that if they did separate we should adopt the baby, but Mrs Evans told my wife that, if they did separate, his mother would take the baby. At a later period, Mrs Evans told me that her husband was knocking her about and that she was going to make an end of it, meaning that she was going to commit suicide.

'One morning shortly after this, it would be early in November, I went upstairs and found Mrs Evans lying on a quilt in front of the fireplace in the kitchen. She had made an attempt to gas herself, and I opened the door and window wide because there was a lot of gas in the room.

'There was a gas pipe on the left-hand side of the fireplace with a tap about 2ft 6in from the floor, about the level of the top of the kitchen fireplace. There was a piece of rubber tubing from the tap near her head. She was lying with her head towards the window. She was fully dressed and was not covered over with anything. When I opened the door and window she started coming round. I gave her a drink of water.

'I don't know what she said, but a little while after she complained of a headache, and I made her a cup of tea. My wife was downstairs, but I did not call her or tell her. Mrs Evans asked me not to tell anyone. Mr Evans was out and I don't know if there was anyone else in the house. I had a cup of tea, too, because my head was thumping as I had got the effect of it too. After a while, I went downstairs.'

Christie said he went upstairs again the next day. Beryl begged him to help her commit suicide, he claimed. She told him she would do anything if he would help her. Christie took that to mean he could be intimate with her.

'She brought the quilt from the front room and put it down in front of the fireplace. I am not sure whether there was a fire in the grate. She lay on the quilt. She was fully dressed. I got on my knees but found I was not physically capable of having intercourse with her, owing to the fact that I had fibrositis in my back and had enteritis.'

Christie said he turned on the gas tap and held it close to her face. When she became unconscious, he turned the tap off.

'I was going to try again to have intercourse with her but it was impossible. I couldn't bend over. I think that's when I strangled her. I think it was with a stocking I found in the room. The gas wasn't on very long, not much more than a minute, I think. Perhaps one or two minutes. I then left her where she was and went downstairs. I think my wife was downstairs. She didn't know anything about it.'

Christie then described his meeting with Evans:

'Evans came home in the evening about six o'clock. It was dark when I heard him come in. I spoke to him in the passage and told him that his wife had committed suicide, that she had gassed herself. I went upstairs with him. We went into the kitchen, and Evans touched his wife's hand, then picked her up and carried her into the bedroom and put her on the bed. It was dark, and there were no lights on in the kitchen or the bedroom.'

Christie said that Evans then fetched a quilt from the kitchen and put it over her. Christie warned Evans that he would be a suspect because of the rows and fights he had had with his wife. Evans thought the same, and said he would take her away somewhere in his van.

Christie said he then left the room and went downstairs, assuming that Evans would take Beryl's body away.

'When I left Evans in the bedroom on that Tuesday evening he did not know that his wife had been strangled. He thought that she had gassed herself. I never mentioned it to him. I never had sexual intercourse with Mrs Evans at any time. We were just friendly acquaintances. I feel certain I strangled Mrs Evans and I think it was with a stocking. I did it because she appealed to me to help her commit suicide. I have got it in the back on my mind that I don't know anything about what happened to the Evans baby. I don't recollect seeing the baby on Tuesday or at any time afterwards. The pubic hairs found in the tin at 10 Rillington Place came from the three women in the alcove and from my wife.'

The tin discovered by police in Christie's flat contained pubic hairs from four sources. There was no positive evidence as to where they had each come from. Christie could have killed many more women during those bleak war years and collected their pubic hair, but we will never know. We can only take Christie's word as to who those four hairs belonged to; and he did not claim that any of them belonged to Beryl, because he knew he had not killed her.

Beryl's young body had already been ravaged by murder and autopsies before Timothy Evans's trial. But now, following Christie's shameless claims, his defence lawyers insisted that her body be exhumed and subjected once more to extensive and unnecessary examinations and procedures. What peace was there for my sister?

The request from Christie's defence was granted, and on Monday, 18 May 1953, Beryl Evans was exhumed and disinterred at 5.30am at Gunnersbury Cemetery in the Royal Borough of Kensington. It was standard to conduct such procedures in the early morning, as it was a 'quiet and private' time. Because the case had attracted a great deal of public attention, special measures were put in place to keep out the public and press: barricades were erected, the cemetery was closed to unauthorised visitors, and 30 police officers were drafted in. However, in spite of this, numerous newspaper reporters and photographers with long-range cameras positioned themselves on the embankment along the Bath Road beside many onlookers, hoping to get a glimpse. This was no ordinary operation.

Christie's lawyers were determined to prove that Christie had killed Beryl Evans to fit his plea of insanity. The prosecution argued, however, that Christie could not be insane, because he had concealed his crimes for years, showing that he knew his actions were wrong. He was of sound mind, but simply had no moral compass.

The pathologists for the exhumation were Dr Donald Teare and Professors Camps and Simpson, affectionately known as 'The Three Musketeers' because they often worked together. Simpson represented the accused, while Camps was nominated to carry out the post-mortem examination. Teare was present as he had carried out the original autopsies on Beryl and Geraldine Evans in December 1949. Jack Abbott Hobson, a psychiatrist, acted for the defence.

The cemetery workers had already lifted the headstone, and the grave was opened to a depth of approximately five feet. The coffin lay on top of six others in a common grave, which in those days would have been dug by hand.

The coffin lid, once cleaned, exposed the breast plate, which was photographed by the police. Once the coffin had been loosened at the sides, it was lifted out.

The coffin of Beryl and Geraldine during the exhumation. Credit: Met Police.

The coffin was identified by the gravedigger, mortuary super-intendent and undertaker. The breast plate read: Beryl Evans, aged 19.

On 8 November 1949, she had actually turned 20 – this was correctly recorded on the headstone. The name of her daughter was misspelt as 'Jeraldine', recorded incorrectly as 14 months old rather than 13 months.

The coffin was in good condition after three years. It was made of one-inch elm boarding and 'kerfed': it was cut in such a way that the wood was allowed to bend. It was requested that the lid should be raised slightly to allow the release of gases before removal from the cemetery.

At 8.15am the 'select committee' assembled at Kensington Mortuary, consisting of L.C. Nickolls, director of the Metropolitan Police Laboratory, Chief Inspector George Salter, Scotland Yard Liaison Officer, and Chief Inspector George Jennings, who had originally taken down Timothy Evans's confession and charged him with the murders of Beryl and Geraldine Evans three years earlier. He had also identified Beryl and Geraldine's bodies at their autopsies.

It was accepted that their exhumation had no bearing on the Evans case, which was officially filed as solved.

Much of this procedure was to be a repeat of the first post-mortem examination in December 1949, but this time it was mainly to establish whether Beryl had been gassed at the time of her murder, as Christie claimed.

The coffin was fully opened. Beryl and Geraldine had been buried together in one coffin. It was the job of Chief Inspector Jennings to identify them for the second time. To everyone's surprise, this proved remarkably easy, as the bodies were still well preserved. The explanation for this was that the weather at the time of death was unusually cold; the bodies had been left in the wash house and later buried in the well-drained sandy soil of the common grave, ensuring that they were still well defined.

Parts of Beryl's thighs were cherry pink in colour. It was agreed that tissue specimens would be taken and tested for traces of carbon monoxide to establish whether Christie had gassed my sister. There was a certain confidence that, as before, this would produce negative results.

The 'cherry pink' colour soon began to fade due to contact with air. Had there been carbon monoxide involved, as Christie suggested, then the cherry pink colour would not have faded.

Camps proceeded to reopen the body by cutting Teare's original sutures. On inspection, those present were surprised once more by how well preserved the exposed organs were, with the lungs still easily identifiable. Just like the other areas, these were cherry pink, but again faded after exposure to the air.

Teare's previous findings were upheld for the heart, and other organs still gave evidence to the fact that Beryl's cause of death was asphyxia.

They then set about removing the uterus, vagina and vulva, which to their surprise came away in one piece, complete with the pubic hair, just as Teare had observed three years previously. Amazingly, it was still clear to see, after taking measurements, that the uterus had been in a pregnant state and that the two marks on the posterior vaginal wall were still identifiable by Teare as the recorded scar and bruise. It was also noted that no pubic hair had been cut.

Because four teeth had been found in the garden of Rillington Place, not belonging to either of the two skeletons buried there, it was arranged for Beryl's jaws and teeth to be sent to a lecturer in dental pathology, Bernard Sims, at the London Hospital. Camps noticed that the crowns of Beryl's teeth were cherry pink. Although this had been observed on other occasions where no carbon monoxide was evident, it nevertheless called for further analysis.

Sixteen jars containing material were retained for laboratory examination, each being sealed by Salter and duly labelled.

Professor Simpson, for the defence, approved the reburial of Beryl's body and that of baby Geraldine. Both were put back in the coffin, to be reinterred the same evening.

The main object of the exercise was to establish if carbon monoxide was present in the body tissue. Teare had established conclusively, the first time, that it wasn't, and the second autopsy produced identical results. The constant dwelling on unidentified pubic hair samples, regarded as 'Christie's trophies', was to take up a great deal of time during the trial and achieve very little.

The exhumation was a sickening and callous event. It was enormously distressing to know that a second autopsy was being carried out on my much-loved sister, given that the well-respected Teare had already drawn his conclusions in 1949. But due to the law around murder charges, Timothy Evans had been convicted only of Geraldine's murder, and this had left the door open for Beryl's case to be re-examined and her dead body mutilated.

To add to our pain as a family, the breast plate from Beryl's coffin was removed during the exhumation on 18 May 1953, and was never replaced. The breast plate, so precious as a means of identifying a loved one, was thoughtlessly treated as a 'souvenir', and now resides somewhere in Scotland Yard's Crime Museum.

The case had taken an even more disturbing turn. And soon John Reginald Halliday Christie was to follow in the footsteps of Timothy John Evans, into the dock at the Old Bailey.

Chapter 19
Christie on Trial

The day of reckoning had come. On Monday, 22 June 1953, in Court Number 1, where he had given evidence against Evans three years previously, Christie himself stood accused of murder.

As with Evans, he could only face the one charge: that of murdering his wife. The members of the jury were reminded that, despite all the publicity surrounding 10 Rillington Place, they had to ignore what they had read and only consider the evidence presented to them in relation to Ethel's death. Naturally, however, details of the other murders were to emerge as the case progressed.

The judge for the case was Oxford-educated Mr Justice Finnemore. The prosecution was led by the Attorney General, Sir Lionel Heald, QC. Derek Curtis-Bennett, QC, represented Christie.

Heald recounted all the evidence and statements, pointing out that Christie actually admitted the charge of murder.

Christie knew what he was doing, Heald told the jury, and he knew it was an illegal act. 'Can you have any possible doubt,' he asked them, 'that Christie deliberately killed his wife on the morning of 14 December?'

Curtis-Bennett, defending Christie, tried to claim that Christie was insane under the so-called 'M'Naghten Rules'. In 1843 Daniel M'Naghten had been acquitted on a murder charge; he thought he had shot the Prime Minister, Sir Robert Peel, but instead his victim was Edward Drummond, Sir Robert's secretary. It was established that M'Naghten was suffering from insane delusions when he shot Mr Drummond, and he was admitted to a lunatic asylum. The judge in the case was Sir Nicolas Conyngham Tindal, better known as Lord Tindal. His guidance, after lengthy debate in legal circles, became a cornerstone in law:

'To establish a defence on the grounds of insanity, it must be clearly proved that, at the time of committing the act, the party accused was labouring under such a defect of reason from disease of the mind, as not to know the nature and quality of the act he was doing, or if he did know it, that he did not know that what he was doing was wrong.'

Curtis-Bennett told the jury repeatedly that Christie was insane, and should not be hanged. Surely, he argued, Christie had to be responsible for the murder of Beryl, too? 'One wonders about the possibilities of there being two stranglers living in the same tiny premises in Notting Hill.'

He continued: 'What man who is not mad goes about strangling women and having intercourse with them after death? What man keeps collections of pubic hairs who is not mad? What man who in fact has gone through a period of three and a half years when he is unable to speak is not starting on the road to insanity? What man could leave the bodies in that house and let the premises to people who ought to have smelt it in five minutes, and who is not an insane man? What man goes around afterwards covered in identification marks who is not mad? I ask from you at the end of this case that you should find this man guilty of the act but insane at the time.'

The Christie I knew was a sane man, and the prosecution too maintained that Christie was sane. Sir Lionel Heald told the jury two eminent doctors had concluded that Christie knew, when he committed murder, that what he was doing was wrong. Had there been a policeman in the vicinity the morning Ethel was murdered, then he would not have killed her.

Mr Justice Finnemore, summing up, explained carefully the decision the jury had to make in such an extraordinary case:

'You will consider this case, the whole of the circumstances of this case, the whole of the evidence we have had, the evidence of the man himself and the history of the crimes, and then consider the one question you have to ask yourselves: is it reasonably probable that when he killed his wife, Mrs Christie, he was suffering from the disease of the mind producing a defect of reason, so that if he knew what he was doing he did not know that it was wrong? Hold the scales of justice equally and decide solely on the view you have formed on the evidence that has been given before you over the last few days in the witness box.

'The mere fact that a man acts like a monster cruelly and wickedly is not of itself evidence that he is insane.'

He added that perhaps no jury in this country had seen a man, charged with murder, go into the witness box and say: 'Yes, I did kill this victim and I killed six others over a period of 10 years.'

On 25 June, just after 4pm, the jury retired to consider their verdict.

While they were pondering the case, Christie casually asked court officials about the cricket score. England were playing Australia in an Ashes test match at Lord's.

The jury returned 80 minutes later, and heard the question from the Clerk of the Court: 'Do you find the prisoner at the Bar, John Reginald Halliday Christie, guilty or not guilty?'

'We find him guilty.'

'You find him guilty, and that is the verdict of you all?'

'It is the verdict of us all.'

Christie was asked if he had anything to say. He said nothing and showed no emotion, although it was noticed that his white knuckles gripped the bar and he shuddered slightly.

Mr Justice Finnemore carefully put on his black cap. The chilling words, read out to Timothy Evans three years earlier, were now addressed to John Reginald Halliday Christie.

'The sentence of the court upon you is that you will be taken from this place to a lawful prison and thence to a place of execution and there you will suffer death by hanging, and that your body be buried within the precincts of the prison in which you shall have last been confined before your execution. And may the Lord have mercy on your soul. Amen.'

Albert Pierrepoint was to be called into action yet again.

Chapter 20
The Scott Henderson Inquiry

Christie was found guilty of murder and sentenced to death, but his trial raised doubts as to whether Timothy Evans had really been responsible for killing my sister Beryl three years earlier. Although Beryl's exhumation and second autopsy should have put these doubts to bed, the shocking extent of Christie's crimes had convinced many in the media and the public that he must have been the man behind all the horrors of 10 Rillington Place.

To address these doubts, on 6 July 1953, it was announced in Parliament by the Home Secretary, Sir David Maxwell Fyfe, that there would be a special inquiry. It would be headed by Mr John Scott Henderson QC to investigate whether the hanged Timothy Evans had really been guilty of Beryl's murder. Scott Henderson would be assisted by Mr George Blackburn, the Assistant Chief Constable of West Riding.

The investigation was popular with both sides of the House, although there was some dissatisfaction because the inquiry was not to be an open one. Henderson, a lawyer, would conduct it in private, assisted by Blackburn, a police officer. The reason for the privacy was the possibility that they would have to question Christie, a convicted murderer; any publicity around this might deter crucial witnesses from attending.

The inquiry report needed to be completed before Christie's execution, scheduled for 15 July 1953. The reason for the hurry was given by the Home Secretary: he 'didn't like to keep a condemned man alive'.

Much of the inquiry was spent interviewing relevant people, including Christie. He was seen at Pentonville Prison by Assistant Chief Constable Blackburn on 8 July 1953. Christie confirmed that he was willing to see Scott Henderson, who interviewed him at the prison the next day.

Christie stated that someone had told him 'there was no proof of him killing Beryl Evans'. He said that if he was given proof that he had killed Beryl and the baby, he would have to admit it.

Further questioning of Christie showed him to be somewhat indecisive. He claimed he couldn't remember killing his wife, the other women in the alcove or the other two buried in the garden, but said that 'I must have done'.

Scott Henderson asked him about the six bodies found at 10 Rillington Place: given that there were four in the house and two in the garden, did he not consider this sufficient proof that he had killed them?

Christie replied: 'Well, it is difficult to say − I am not convinced about it − it is obvious that I did.'

And so he went on in a similar pattern.

He was then asked once more about the death of Beryl Evans. Again, he was not sure, suggesting that if someone came up with definite proof of his killing Beryl Evans, he would accept it as being right, and that he wanted to know the truth of the matter too. He kept insisting: 'I was only informed yesterday that there is no such proof.'

Throughout Scott Henderson's interview, Christie would not admit whether or not he had killed any of the people found on the premises of 10 Rillington Place.

We know that Christie had 'invented' his confession about killing Beryl in order to enter a plea of insanity; now that this had been rejected and he had been convicted of Ethel's murder, he seemed to be distancing himself from Beryl's death once more. He was reluctant to reiterate his confession. Moreover, he firmly denied the murder of baby Geraldine right to the very end.

In due course Scott Henderson presented his report on the Evans trial and murder conviction. A Supplementary Report (Section 49) summarises his findings:

1. The case for the prosecution against Evans as presented to the jury at his trial was an overwhelming one.

2. Having considered all of the material now available relating to the deaths of Mrs Evans and Geraldine Evans, I am satisfied that there can be no doubt that Evans was responsible for both.

3. Christie's statements that he was responsible for the death of Mrs Evans were not only unreliable but were untrue.

Scott Henderson detailed the evidence given by the police officers about Timothy Evans's 'confession'. He was satisfied that no details relating to the bodies or causes of death had been divulged to Evans before his confession, other than in the evidence given by Chief Inspector Jennings at his trial. Therefore, Evans could not have known the details unless he had first-hand knowledge of their murders by strangulation and the concealment of their bodies.

Throughout the entire case, dates and times had always been inconclusive, particularly with the workmen, who never seemed sure of anything, despite having worksheets. The inquiry understood from the workmen's employers that the back wall of the recess and the W.C. were repointed during 9, 10 and 11 November. Scott Henderson was incorrect when he said that, after 8 November, the plasterer worked inside the house. The employers stated that the plasterer would have continued working in the yard, and inside and outside the wash house. They were drawing water, mixing materials and accessing tools where they had been stored throughout the works.

Henderson made the necessary checks of timesheets by the employers from 1948 until 1953 inclusive. They confirmed that all had been accounted for, apart from plasterers' records from 1 to 11 November 1949. The employers said these had not been handed back to them. Surely the wages were calculated on the strength of timesheets? The inquiry should have been given time to carry out an in-depth investigation into the missing documents.

As far as the evidence is concerned, the plasterer collected his tools and swept up on the Saturday morning of 12 November 1949. What is certain, then, is that neither body could have been put in the wash house until the completion of all works and the full clearance of the site when the leftover timber was given to Christie.

The newspaper cutting found in Rillington Place, about the Stanley Setty torso murder, was seen as further proof that Evans's guilty verdict was correct. There was some speculation that Christie had planted the cutting there, to incriminate Evans, but this is implausible. Planting a cutting about another case was not something that the Christie I knew would do. For me, the newspaper cutting didn't prove anything; the Setty murder was an enormous case at the time and, although he wasn't the best reader, Evans was no doubt fascinated by the story. The whole country was intrigued.

Scott Henderson stated that the murders were 'unpremeditated'. On this point, I would disagree: both murders most certainly were premeditated. My beloved sister and niece were both stran-gled, one with a rope – which, by Evans's own admission, he had brought in from his van – and one with a tie. Timothy Evans had physically and mentally abused Beryl on numerous occasions and threatened to kill her. As for baby Geraldine, she just got in his way.

The inquiry was given a very short time to prepare a report. All it seemed to produce was repetition of previously exhausted words and phrases.

Twenty-four people gave statements, though none of them were named in the report. This was an oversight: had some of the state-ments been submitted by the prosecution at the time of the Evans trial, a more comprehensive understanding of Timothy Evans's violent nature and compulsive lying would have been evident.

As it was, the true character of Timothy Evans remained little understood. The report received a critical reception in Parliament, as many remained sympathetic to Evans, knowing nothing of his long history of violence and deceit.

Alongside this, the following important facts should have been emphasised: no abortion was carried out, Beryl was not gassed, and there was no trace of sexual intercourse. The deaths of Beryl and Geraldine took place in totally different circumstances.

It is clear that Evans was the killer in both cases.

Chapter 21
Christie and the Hangman

On 15 July 1953, expert hangman Albert Pierrepoint was called upon to carry out the execution of another Rillington Place tenant. Having hanged Timothy John Evans on 9 March 1950, his services were required once more, to end the life of John Reginald Halliday Christie.

The evening before the execution Pierrepoint, in his usual fashion, observed the condemned man in the prison yard. Pierrepoint remarked that Christie did not seem downcast; he was striding confidently between two death watch officers. Pierrepoint said Christie's eyes were glinting sharply behind his spectacles, beneath the carefully combed wisps of hair on that big domed head.

Christie made no appeal and concentrated instead on sorting out his paperwork. He made out a will, leaving all he had to his sister, Phyllis Halliday Clarke. He wrote in the document that he apologised for any trouble he might have brought about.

As his execution drew nearer, Christie received two visitors. One was a comrade from the First World War. After an exchange of letters, Dennis Hague visited on 13 July. They discussed their early years, and Christie had the usual memory loss about his crimes. Christie viewed Hague as an utterly dejected, lonely and broken man.

His sister Phyllis visited the day before the hanging, and reported that he didn't seem at all downcast. He told her: 'Don't worry about the morning. They won't hurt me. They'll take my glasses off before they hang me, so I won't see much.'

The governor also visited Christie on the eve of the hanging; the condemned man had nothing to say. Rev William George Morgan, the Anglican chaplain at the prison, talked to Christie; his impression was that Christie had definitely not killed Geraldine and most probably did not strangle Beryl.

As the time drew nearer to 9am on 15 July, though, Christie had an alcoholic drink as he prepared to plunge through the trapdoor.

It was rare for Christie to drink. I never saw him take any alcohol – only tea. I knew that he drank very little, just the occasional pint of beer. He might have had something stronger at Christmas, but even then it would be just a glass or two.

We don't know what it was that he drank, but he certainly took a gulp in his final five minutes.

Pierrepoint left his room at Pentonville, followed closely by his assistant for the day, Harry Smith. Pierrepoint described the hanging scene:

'Christie had his back to the door when I went in. He was listening with a tight-lipped little sneer to the low, consoling words of the chaplain. As I motioned towards the execution chamber, all Christie's face seemed to melt. It was more than terror. I think it was not that he was afraid of the act of execution. He had lived with and gloated upon corpses. But I knew in that moment that John Reginald Christie would have given anything in his power to postpone the moment of death. My assistant and I had his skimpy wrists pinioned before he knew fully what was happening, and then he rose to his feet, a little taller than I was, so that I had to reach up to remove his spectacles.

'In that instant I met his eyes and quite slowly pulled off his glasses, laying them carefully upon the scrubbed bone table beside me. This was his last moment to speak. He blinked bewilderingly, screwing up his eyes. Then he focussed them on the door that stood open between the condemned cell and the execution chamber.'

Pierrepoint observed that Christie's normally combed hair was untidy; there was no need for vanity on this occasion. Christie faltered pitifully, not so much walking as drifting forwards. His legs stumbled and it looked as if he was going to faint.

'My nose is itchy,' Christie is said to have told him, unable to move his arms, of course.

'It won't bother you for long,' Pierrepoint reassured the condemned man.

Pierrepoint pulled the lever, and it was all over.

'I hanged John Reginald Christie, the "Monster of Rillington Place", in less time than it took the ash to fall off a cigar I had left half-smoked in my room at Pentonville.'

More than 200 people were waiting outside the prison gates for news. The announcement of Christie's death was placed on the prison gates at just after 9.05am. Onlookers described a commotion, with plenty of cheering and jeering.

The crowds shared information about the case and how many people Christie had killed. Rillington Place was on everyone's tongue.

So Evans was innocent after all, they concluded.

Some of those who had seen the notice headed off to 10 Rillington Place, where they stood and stared at the infamous building, much to the annoyance of the local residents.

Notting Hill had finally got rid of two evil murderers. For ever.

Chapter 22
Peter and Lea

Ten years on from the Christie trial, in 1963, I was running the Thorley School of Motoring in Brighton. I was driving along in my Austin Cambridge one day when I spotted one of my pupils, Paul, walking up from the beach alongside an attractive woman. I wound down the window to say hello. Paul introduced his fiancée, Lea, and said she was looking to have driving lessons as well. Lea was staying in Brighton because her family had pubs in the area, while Paul was a cabinet maker, about 18 months older than her.

'Will next Wednesday suit you?' I suggested quickly.

I liked Lea straight away and I knew she liked me. She wasn't particularly interested in learning to drive – we enjoyed our lessons more as a way of spending time together. She was 17 and I was 11 years older. The age gap didn't matter to either of us.

After our first lesson, Paul was amicably sidelined. He didn't get too upset, although he had lost a gem.

I was enjoying getting to know Lea, but I knew I needed to disclose my past to her. As it happened, after one lesson Lea mentioned a murder case she'd seen in the local paper, *The Evening Argus*. There we were, sitting in the front of the car, and I took my opportunity.

'Lea, I've got something to tell you.'

'Go on, you're married already!'

'No, nothing like that.'

'You're not really a driving instructor.'

'No, it's something really serious.'

'Try me.'

'I just thought the time was right, with you talking about that murder case in the paper…'

'Eh?'

'Well, do you remember the Rillington Place murders?'

'Yes it was in all the papers. They hanged two people? They didn't get anybody for the murder of a woman…'

'Yes, she was called Beryl. Beryl Evans was my sister.'

The gravity of the situation was evident, looking at Lea. Her jaw dropped and she stared at me, trying to take everything in. I could see she was going over what she remembered, with all the bodies being found at the house.

'There was a young child, murdered as well?'

'That was my niece, Geraldine. My sister's baby girl. Timothy Evans was hanged, but it was only for Geraldine's murder, although it was assumed he killed them both. Then it turned out that Reg Christie in the house had killed several women and now people think he killed Beryl and Geraldine as well.

'I grew up with them both, and I know Evans was guilty of killing Beryl and the baby. It's a lot for you to get your head around. Evans and Christie were both hanged three years apart by the same hangman. It's a sordid tale. It's a lot of baggage, I'm so sorry.'

'That's a lot to take in,' Lea answered thoughtfully.

I had played all my cards. I had to tell her. I needed to tell Lea everything because that gave her the opportunity to stop the relationship and move on. I pressed on with my revelations.

'Another thing is, I need to get to the bottom of what really happened. It's on my mind every day and I need to keep finding out more and more to get to the truth. They're still saying that Christie killed Beryl and Geraldine. But it was Evans, I know that. How do you feel now?'

'I'm intrigued.' She smiled. 'Looks like we're in it together for the long run!'

A few months later, when I went to see Lea to celebrate her 18th birthday, I had an engagement ring in its box in my pocket. In the evening, I went round to her family's pub in Brighton, the Dolphin Inn in North Road, to hand over her birthday present. I had chosen a pair of sparkling stiletto heels for her. Another 'sparkler' was about to head in her direction.

'Here,' I said, throwing the ring across the room, like the true romantic that I was. 'You may as well have this as well!'

As Lea tried on the ring, so excited, it suddenly brought back to me the great sadness of that day in Rillington Place when Beryl handed me her wedding ring. It was such a contrast in emotions. There I was, looking at the delight on Lea's face when she received her ring. And yet, in my mind, all I saw was the sadness and despair on Beryl's face as she had handed me her ring – to stop her cruel husband selling it.

Lea and I have led a varied, interesting and happy life together. We married in 1965, right in the middle of 'flower power'. When you went to a party, it was standing or laying room only; you had a glass of lemonade, breathed normally and felt as high as a kite. As I ran a driving school, I could hardly have anything in my lemonade, though of course that didn't apply to Lea.

The 1950s dull fashions had gone, to be replaced with loose, colourful clothes and psychedelic designs. Scott McKenzie in 1967 was singing *'If you're going to San Francisco, be sure to wear some flowers in your hair'*. That year saw the *'Summer of Love'*, featuring The Who, The Mamas and the Papas, Jimi Hendrix and so many more top acts. The pinnacle had to be the Beatles LP *Sergeant Pepper's Lonely Hearts Club Band*.

We ran a chauffeur business down in Brighton. We ferried a lot of the pop stars around to Gatwick, Heathrow, London theatres and wherever they wanted to go. I drove Cliff Richard,

Adam Faith, Eartha Kitt, Vera Lynn, Bryan Ferry and many more. Vera Lynn was lovely, a real lady, and I could see why she was known as the 'Forces' Sweetheart'. I also liked Bryan Ferry. He was really chatty and would talk to me about anything under the sun while he sat there humming away with his girl singers in the back of the limousine. It was a real privilege to be in the company of international superstars.

After that, Lea and I ran a restaurant in Rottingdean – a proper fish restaurant with fresh daily catches from the local fishing ports. Lea was the chef and I served as the waiter. We were involved in other businesses, too, and always interested in new ventures.

Lea was an only child, but always said she enjoyed a happy childhood surrounded by a loving family. But, with the family in business, times could be lonely and she vowed she would never have just one child when it came to having offspring.

We had five. Lea prefers to say it was three plus twins, so it doesn't sound like a small army. We had no idea the twins were coming. They were not spotted until the day of delivery.

We have amazing, loving, caring kids and we are proud of them all: Martin, Jo, Rachel, and twins Peter and Lea, who are still our babies. And now we also have four gorgeous grandchildren and four great-grandchildren, which makes a houseful.

Lea was always so supportive as I began to investigate the truth of what really happened to Beryl and Geraldine. As our family grew older, they all came to realise the hurt and anguish we suffered. Still today, some dates in the year are spent in mourning. The birthdays of Beryl and Geraldine, and the dates of their deaths, are days when Lea and I pause, reflect and remember two very special people. Their lives were cut short by Timothy Evans.

I knew, deep in my heart, that justice would catch up with him eventually. He was rightly hanged, because of the overwhelming evidence against him but, sadly, that was far from the end of the Evans story.

Chapter 23
Rillington Place On Screen

The murders at Rillington Place had shocked and horrified the nation, and rumours continued to circle about what had really happened to Beryl and Geraldine. The most popular theories emerged in a book by Ludovic Kennedy, *Ten Rillington Place*, which came out in 1961 and led to the film of the same name, *10 Rillington Place*.

The film was made in 1970 and premiered in the UK on 28 January 1971. It went on general release in May. Richard Attenborough played the role of Christie, with John Hurt portraying Evans and Judy Geeson taking on the role of Beryl.

All three actors were superb. Attenborough, although shorter than Christie, came across as extremely sinister. It wasn't as I remembered Christie, but Attenborough 'owned' the part. An article in *The Times* described his appearance in the street as 'chilling', and those who had lived there during the time of the murders found him disturbingly convincing.

Speaking later, Attenborough said: 'It was a very difficult film to make. It could be in appalling bad taste; it could be ludicrously macabre; it could be a cri de coeur or a moral question and not a piece of cinema. Dick Fleischer, the director, turned it into a piece of cinema.'

John Hurt looked not dissimilar to Evans, and really mastered his Welsh accent and limp. He revealed that, during the execution scene, Albert Pierrepoint was brought in as a technical adviser. It was the first time that a British cinema had shown a hanging scene in the UK.

Judy Geeson – despite looking nothing like Beryl – put in a masterful performance. She would just have seen pictures of Beryl, with no idea how she actually talked, but she truly captured the emotion of her character.

She said later: 'It was a damned good part. I was twenty-something and I approached it as a job that I had to do. I didn't overthink it. We weren't made to look pretty and we weren't in pretty clothes. We were filmed very nicely, but it was raw.'

At the time of the filming, three families were still living at 10 Rillington Place and unwilling to move out, so No. 7 was used instead. The traditional grey-and-green colour scheme was used, while front doors from the period were installed in the houses.

Vehicles from the 1940s and 1950s were used, with signs for air-raid shelters on the streets. There are telephone cables visible, though, which only appeared in real life long after Christie's reign of terror.

Unfortunately, both Ludovic Kennedy's book and the film deviated wildly from the truth of what really happened at 10 Rillington Place. Unmoved by the overwhelming burden of proof against Timothy Evans, both the book and the film sought to exonerate him for the murder of my sister Beryl, laying the blame at the feet of Reg Christie instead. Nowhere in the film is there an accurate account of Evans's true disposition. There is no reference to the fact that he was a compulsive liar with an uncontrollable temper, capable of extreme violence.

The film was undoubtedly sensationalised for commercial benefit. Reg is presented as 'back street abortionists', and it is while performing an abortion on Beryl that Reg Christie murders her.

There is no evidence that Reg Christie performed abortions, or even that he had any medical knowledge. In the film, Christie produces a medical book to show off his knowledge; he also has some framed medical certificates for first aid. This is a bizarre twisting of the truth: Christie had no medical qualifications. I spent hours inside his house, and there were no framed certificates or medical books to speak of. In reality, the Christies had commented how ill Beryl was looking following her attempts to self-abort, and they wanted to dissuade her from any more risky attempts to terminate her pregnancy.

As much as Beryl might not have wanted another baby, there is no way she would have discussed abortion with Reg Christie or believed in his ability to carry out the termination. There was never any impropriety between Christie and Beryl Evans in real life. What's more, Evans would surely not have agreed to his wife having an abortion carried out by Christie. The film's depiction of Christie discussing an abortion with Beryl is totally fabricated. It is merely a means of making the theory of Christie's guilt more plausible.

The murder scene begins with Evans coming downstairs on his way to work, telling Christie that Beryl is ready for him to carry out the abortion. Christie sends his wife Ethel off to his workplace to tell them he is unwell – presumably in order to 'get her out of the way'. He then goes to his 'medical cabinet', affixed to the wall in the kitchen – which in reality was just a kitchen dresser containing plates and crockery.

Christie takes from the cabinet various paraphernalia including a piece of rubber tubing, a crudely-made mask and a short length of rope, which he places in a briefcase. He pours a cup of tea. Then he heads upstairs, ready to carry out the abortion.

He is stopped in his tracks when the doorbell rings. Even this is a certain departure from the truth. There was no doorbell at 10 Rillington Place – there was no electricity or batteries to power one with. It was an old-fashioned knocker.

Christie dithers, cup of tea in hand, briefcase under his arm, and gingerly goes to the door, which he opens. Three workmen, addressing him as 'Mr Christie', announce that they are from the council and will be carrying out work on the wash house roof. He tells them it is inconvenient, but condescends to allow them in, letting them through to the back, still with cup and saucer in hand. This, again, is an impossible scenario, dreamt up by a scriptwriter: the work had actually started a week before that, on 31 October.

Christie comes back indoors into his kitchen and proceeds to pour out another cup of tea from the same pot. The front door is left open for the workmen to have access. As he goes upstairs Beryl appears at the top, making sure everything is all right. He goes in and offers her the cup of tea.

Christie brings an eiderdown from the bedroom, which he lays on the kitchen floor near a gas pipe. Beryl, standing by the kitchen window, sees the workmen and hears them sawing.

Christie tells her to 'open the window six inches' and pull the blinds.

Christie gets ready to perform the illegal abortion. He gasses Beryl to relax her; Beryl panics and struggles. Christie punches her twice in the face with the full force of his fist, rendering her unconscious.

After that, he rapes and strangles her.

With the bedroom window open, why do none of the workmen hear her scream?

The film fails to acknowledge the fact that Christie was an intelligent man. He would never have taken such chances, given the time and circumstances of the day. Committing murder with the front door open, workmen in the house, and a window open, was out of the question for a man of his methods.

We are given to understand Christie has explained the risks associated with abortion to Evans and Beryl, warning them that one in 10 die during the operation. When Timothy Evans comes home from work in the evening, Christie is waiting for him. 'It's bad news, Tim.'

Evans asks where Beryl is, and is told that she is lying on the bed.

At this point, baby Geraldine must still be in her cot in the only bedroom. If the order of events in the film were true, she would have spent most of the day alone, and by now would be crying incessantly.

Christie tells Evans to go upstairs, and follows him up.

They go into the bedroom, where Beryl is lying on the bed, partially covered with an eiderdown. Evans looks at her. There is no evidence of injuries consistent with the two hefty blows to her face that Christie supposedly delivered; there is only a small amount of blood in the region of her chin. Christie justifies this by saying she hit her head on the corner of the bed when she struggled.

Evans says there is some blood from the 'lower part of her body'. However, he completely overlooks the clearly visible 'rope burn' around her neck. Evans then exclaims: 'She's not alive, Mr Christie, she's dead! Should we get a doctor?'

If this was how events truly played out, how could Evans not notice the rope burn around his wife's neck, or the bruising on her legs?

The film's portrayal of Evans's reaction is utterly implausible and bizarre. Evans comes home from work to find that his wife has been murdered by Christie, following an attempt to abort her. His baby daughter Geraldine is still in her cot where she has been all day, alongside the bed where the body of her mother, Beryl, is lying.

Evans, sobbing, holds a lengthy conversation with Christie, taking in the whys and wherefores of the day's tragic events and where they both stand in respect of the law. Christie then suggests that he should feed his daughter. After all, he has been at work all day and she must be hungry. Christie then says they will have to discuss what to do next.

If Evans was truly innocent, as the film suggests, then this was his opportunity to leave the house. Knowing that he couldn't deal with baby Geraldine alone, why didn't he take her to the safety of his mother's home, a mere two minutes' walk away in St Mark's Road? Alternatively, he could have gone straight to the police station, only a few hundred yards from there.

In reality, he did not do anything of the sort. His actions after Beryl's death were deliberately evasive and ultimately incriminating.

As with the official inquest into Evans's conviction, Ludovic Kennedy's mistake was to overlook Timothy Evans's true character. He makes Evans out to be a simple, laid-back paragon of virtue. Kennedy portrays Evans as 'the innocent victim' who was wrongly convicted, failing to mention his heavy drinking and gambling as the reason for the couple's shortage of money.

Kennedy did not record the extent of Evans's failings, his lies, drinking, gambling, cheating and extreme violence towards his own wife over a lengthy period. Yet evidence has shown that this was well documented by many: there were occasions when it was stated that Evans's own mother had given him a 'slap' for his treatment of Beryl. Even Lucy Endicott ended her relationship with Evans after a couple of days because of his violence.

Unfortunately, Ludovic Kennedy worked closely with Timothy Evans's family while writing his book, which inevitably led to a favourable portrayal of a man I knew to be deceitful and dangerous. More distressingly, he made no effort to hear the perspective of the victims' families, and described Beryl in deeply offensive and demeaning terms. He failed to mention that Beryl wanted to leave Evans because of his violence, and that our father William visited his daughter on 5 November 1949. He overlooked the fact that Beryl wanted to take Geraldine to Brighton and live with my father.

Kennedy seemed to forget that Beryl and baby Geraldine were the victims in this horrific murder case. He showed no compassion towards anyone but Evans and his family, ignoring the fact that when Evans was first arrested, even his own flesh and blood were well aware of his abhorrent behaviour. He ignored the fact that my sister was a lovely, caring woman who would do anything for anyone, and deserved so much better.

Kennedy described himself as 'committed to revealing hidden truths', but he got so much wrong in *Ten Rillington Place*. Few came out unscathed from his criticism – not even the three highly respected and experienced pathologists Teare, Camps and Simpson, all top professionals who had carried out the second autopsy on Beryl fully and capably. Kennedy also unjustly alleged that Mr Justice Lewis, the judge who presided over the Evans trial, had 'grossly distorted the truth and his summing up was not impartial'.

Finally, Kennedy never explained Evans's motive for murdering Geraldine. In reality, he killed her because she kept screaming. If Evans was innocent of Beryl's murder and couldn't cope with looking after Geraldine alone, he would have picked his child up and taken her to his mother's house around the corner. The fact that he did not is sure proof of his guilty conscience.

I have endured over 70 years of intense sorrow since the murders of my beloved sister and niece, and let us not forget her unborn baby boy, who had no chance of life.

Kennedy's concealment of Evans's true nature was inexcusable. The individuals who might have witnessed or heard about his violence and murderous threats included: Reg and Ethel Christie, Mr and Mrs Vincent, Lucy Endicott, neighbours Mrs

Swan, Mrs Hyde and my father. And Beryl, of course, had told me about his wicked ways many times.

If only more witnesses had been called to the original trial, Kennedy might never have felt the need to defend him in his misguided, misleading, but sadly hugely influential book.

Kennedy was so wrong, but many took his version of events as gospel.

Chapter 24
A Royal Pardon for Evans

Despite the conclusions drawn from the Evans and Christie trials, not to mention Henderson's subsequent inquiry, Ludovic Kennedy's book had an enormous impact on public opinion surrounding the Rillington Place murders. Having seen Kennedy's portrayals of this supposedly innocent man, a campaign to clear Evans's name soon began to gather momentum. Fourteen years on from his death, the Shadow Home Secretary, Frank Soskice, decided there were grounds for another inquiry. When Soskice became Home Secretary in 1964, however, he changed his mind and decided that an inquiry would not serve any useful purpose.

But the wheels had been set in motion nonetheless. A Timothy Evans Committee was formed, and Kennedy himself was appointed as one of the members. Others included leading lawyer and respected investigator Michael Eddowes, who had published a book in 1955 that also argued Evans's innocence, naming Christie as the real culprit. Also on the committee was Harold Evans, who went on to become editor of the *Sunday Times*.

Pressure for an inquiry to go ahead grew and grew, with 113 MPs signing a motion in favour of it. Finding himself under significant pressure, Soskice appointed a High Court Judge, Sir Daniel Brabin, to study the case in more detail and announce his findings.

A total of 79 witnesses were interviewed over two months. Kennedy was one of those who gave his version of events, despite his lack of involvement at the time of the murders. Brabin eventually concluded that, if all the evidence had been made available, no jury would have convicted Evans of the murders of Beryl or Geraldine. He decided that Evans had probably not murdered Geraldine, although he was hanged for that crime. He did, however, think that Evans probably had murdered my sister Beryl.

By 18 October 1966, another Home Secretary, Roy Jenkins, was in place. He was firmer in his opinions than his predecessor, and, to my horror, recommended the granting of a free pardon to Evans.

ELIZABETH THE SECOND, by the Grace of God of the United Kingdom of Great Britain and Northern Ireland and of Our other Realms and Territories Queen, Head of the Commonwealth, Defender of the Faith, To all to whom these Presents shall come Greeting!

A Royal Pardon for Evans

WHEREAS Timothy John Evans at the Central Criminal Court on the thirteenth day of January, 1950, was convicted of murder and sentenced to death;

NOW KNOW YE that We in consideration of some circumstances humbly Represented unto Us, are Graciously pleased to extend Our Grace and Mercy and to grant him Our Free Pardon in respect of the said conviction; and We do hereby command all Justices and others whom it may concern that they take due notice hereof;

And for so doing this shall be a sufficient Warrant

Given at Our Court at St. James's the 18th day of October, 1966, in the year of Our reign.

Roy Jenkins

BY HER MAJESTY'S COMMAND

I was stunned. Timothy Evans had been found guilty of the murder of my niece, and hanged for the crime without ever being tried for the murder of my sister. However, Sir Daniel Brabin thought he did not murder my niece, but probably killed my sister. And suddenly he was granted a royal pardon.

Evans's family tried in vain to have the case referred to the Court of Appeal; they said that the posthumous pardon was an inadequate remedy for Evans's death sentence, and demanded that the conviction should be quashed altogether.

In 2004, the Criminal Cases Review Commission refused to refer the case to the Court of Appeal. There would be 'no tangible benefit to Mr Evans's family, the public interest or the criminal justice system', the Commission said. They argued that the free pardon in 1966 was 'sufficient to establish his innocence and to restore his reputation', given the amount of publicity around the supposed miscarriage of justice. The national media reported that lawyers for Maureen Westlake, Timothy Evans's half-sister, would 'point to the fact that an earlier inquiry, although concluding that Mr Evans probably did not kill his daughter, did not declare him innocent'.

Six months later, Mr Justice Collins and Mr Justice Stanley Burnton would not overturn the Commission's decision. Mr Justice Collins declared that Evans should be regarded as innocent of both murders, but that such a statement in court had no legal standing.

Evans's conviction for murder was never quashed: it still stands to this day. But he is widely regarded as an innocent man.

John Curnow, who wrote a book and runs a website dedicated to *The Murders, Myths and Reality of 10 Rillington Place*, goes into more detail:

> *A royal pardon was granted in October 1966, largely based upon the outcome of the Public Inquiry held under Mr Justice Brabin which reported that year, but his conviction for murder was never quashed and so still stands.*
>
> *The end of the legal road in that regard came in 2004 when the Criminal Cases Review Commission confirmed its earlier decision*

not to refer the case to the Court of Appeal as there would, in their
view, be no practical benefit to be gained from the time and expense
of such proceedings as the pardon had already served effectively
to exonerate the convicted person and restore his reputation in the
public perception, despite not expunging the conviction itself. This
stems from the principle that respects the constitutional distinction
between the roles of the monarch and the court.

Timothy Evans thus retains the dubious privilege of being one
of only two executed criminals ever to be pardoned in England and
Wales – and the only one to have had his conviction remain unquashed.

The myths have grown over the years as to Christie's involvement in the case, but Mr Curnow agrees with me that Christie was not an abortionist. Many have accepted the notion that Christie offered to assist Beryl with her termination in order to gain intimate access to her, and some far-fetched accounts have suggested that he was engaged on a production line basis, assisted by his wife. We know now that this is unsubstantiated nonsense.

Indeed, Detective Chief Inspector Jennings, who was in charge of the Evans inquiry, later declared that Christie was not involved in abortion. He had made a thorough search of the Christies' flat, looking for specific evidence of any such activities, and found nothing. In March 1955 he, together with Black and Griffin, all three now at the rank of Superintendent, went so far as to state this formally. Archived material contains a substantial volume of witness statements from residents of 10 Rillington Place and elsewhere, and in none of these is there any suggestion or allegation made about abortions. If Christie ever did claim otherwise, it was most likely a ruse to gain access to a victim for his true purpose.

Historian Jonathan Oates has written extensively about Christie and Evans and scrutinised the case in the finest detail. He comes to the same conclusion as me, although his dates differ. So many dates were changed in statements; we have no way of knowing exactly when Beryl and Geraldine were killed. Lea and I have established a timeline that we believe to be correct. Here is Jonathan's verdict:

It is commonly believed that Timothy Evans was innocent of murder. There has been a film, a TV drama and several books which state that this is so. It is no surprise, therefore, that most people who know of the case will say this too. It has also been used as an article of faith by opponents of the death penalty. However, we need to look behind the impression given by the media and politics and look at the facts. Even the judicial review of 1965-1966 stated 'it is more probable than not that Timothy Evans killed Beryl Evans'.

On 8 November 1949, Beryl Evans was murdered by strangulation in her rooms at 10 Rillington Place; shortly afterwards her 13-month-old daughter, Geraldine, was strangled with a tie and their bodies were found on 2 December in the outhouse of the said property.

Beryl's husband, Timothy Evans, was charged with the murders, tried for the latter, found guilty and hanged on 9 March 1950. Beryl was last seen alive leaving the property on 8 November and no one saw her re-enter, presumably because she did so after 5pm, after the other occupants, both the Christies downstairs and some workmen, at the house that day, had left.

Frederick Jones, labourer, stated: 'I saw a young woman come downstairs with a baby in her arms and she was accompanied by another young woman. This was the first and last time I saw these people.' The next person to arrive at the house was her husband.

The evidence against Evans is compelling indeed. Evans made a number of confessions to the police. It is usual, if criminals do this, to begin with lies and then to say something approaching the truth. The statement that Evans and his defenders state as being truthful is, when he discovered his wife's body, an impossible one. He stated that 'she had been bleeding from the mouth and nose and that she had been bleeding from the bottom part'. Yet the pathologist, Dr Donald Teare, who examined the corpse, found no evidence of bleeding, but the marks of strangulation around her neck and bruising to the face. If the statement was true, why were there invented details and not the most important part of all?

The rest of the confession is also unconvincing. It shows Evans as a weak and malleable character, but other evidence shows he could be manipulative as he conned one of his employers out of money.

More truthfully, Evans later said: 'I came home at night at about 6.30pm, my wife started to argue again, so I hit her across the face with my flat hand. She then hit me back with her hand. In a fit of temper I grabbed a piece of rope from a chair which I had brought off my van and strangled her with it.'

He later admitted to wrapping her up in a blanket and putting her where she was found.

As to Geraldine, two days later: 'I then went home and picked up my baby from her cot in the bedroom, picked up my tie and strangled her with it.'

Evans was given very little information about the details of the murder: simply that the bodies were found in the wash house. He could not have known what he needed to know to make these confessions unless he was the murderer. Yet he stated that Beryl had been strangled and that she had been wrapped up in a blanket and covered with wood. He knew that Geraldine had been strangled with a tie and hidden behind some wood. Only the killer could have known all these details.

It has been alleged that the final admission of guilt was made under pressure and under threats, but Evans never complained of such; he even referred to one of the policemen as 'a gentleman'. He also made similar confessions off the record to others. To PS Trevallion he said: 'it was the constant crying of the baby that got on my nerves. I just had to strangle her. I just had to put an end to it, I just couldn't put up with the crying.'

When in jail, the prison doctor said Evans had 'an inadequate psychopathic personality, which tends to make him act impulsively with little or no foresight or consideration for others.'

In prison he met another psychopath, murderer Donald Hume. Nine years later, Hume alleged that Evans opened up to him: 'In the presence of several prisoners Evans admitted to killing the baby because it kept crying. So in the presence of these lags and a guard, I hooked him and was booked for it. I have no scruples about adults killing each other, but I dislike people who hurt kids and animals.' There is a reference to a prison officer having to separate Hume and Evans, so this story may well be true and it independently ties up with Trevallion's.

Relations between the Evanses were poor. They were living on the breadline and another baby was on the way. Evans liked drinking and the little family was heavily in debt to a hire purchase company to the tune of £39 13s and £12 1s 6d to their landlord for rent (Evans's weekly wage was between £5 and £6, and more with overtime). Neighbours recalled the two constantly arguing and Beryl was not one to back down from a quarrel; she was a feisty young woman. Evans said: 'She was incurring one debt after another and I could not stand it any longer, so I strangled her with a piece of rope.'

His uncle stated that 'I know Timothy to have a very violent temper' and his half-sister declared that he 'was a bit rough with his temper'. Evans was a violent man and his wife once had to defend herself with a bread knife. He once tried to throw her out of a window and Lucy Endicott once said, having witnessed it first-hand, 'he set about her', and began hitting her with his hand across her face and body. He was in a furious temper and said: 'I'll put you through the bloody window.'

This ties in with Mrs Swan, a neighbour, who saw the Evanses struggling in front of a window, and there is no obvious way that these two witnesses acted in collusion. When Lucy and Evans split up after a brief fling, he said: 'If I ever get hold of Lucy, I'll smash her up or run her over with my lorry.' A violent character indeed.

This ties up with Christie's comment: 'Mrs Evans has told my wife that on more than one occasion he has assaulted her and grabbed hold of her throat.' A neighbour said she thought he was trying to push her out of the window. Lucy said: 'On several occasions I have heard him say to Beryl, 'I'll do you in.' There are so many comments like this from the time.

After he had committed the double murder, he went to his uncle and aunt's house in Wales. He seemed relaxed and happy, sold or gave away items that had belonged to his wife, and went for drinking sessions and sing-songs in the pub. Later, in prison, after conviction, he never became angry or complained that this was a wrongful conviction, nor seemed upset about the demise of his wife and baby. He made no complaint to the hangman or his assistant and the former said: 'I am absolutely certain he was guilty.'

Those who point to Christie as the murderer note that he confessed to killing Beryl but not Geraldine. Yet Christie's confession was nonsense; he stated that he gassed Beryl prior to killing her (as he did with most of his other victims). Yet when she was exhumed there was no evidence that she had been gassed. Since Christie, an intelligent man, wanted to be believed, in order to increase his victim count and thus be thought insane and so escape the gallows ('the more the merrier,' he said), he would have been sure to get his details right. As Dr Camps, pathologist on the case, said of Christie's confession: 'Improbable if not impossible.'

Furthermore, for Christie to have killed Beryl in the afternoon of 8 November would have been impossible for other reasons. First, Beryl would have struggled for her life, and Christie was a weak middle-aged man who needed gas to subdue young women. It seems hard to think he could have subdued her unaided. Secondly, she would have screamed. The noise of that and the fight would have attracted the attention of Mrs Christie and the workmen then employed in the building. Christie could not have done it.

However, on the evening of 8 November, the workmen had gone home. The Christies had left the house, he to the doctor's and she to the public library. There was no one in the house when Evans returned, except his wife and daughter. Lucy noted that Evans did not like his wife being out of the house.

This was a sordid domestic murder. The fact that Evans's downstairs fellow tenant was also a murderer is a coincidence, but these murders did not bear his hallmark, let alone the fact that I believe he was at the doctor's at the time of Beryl's murder. Christie hid his victims rather better and the Evans corpses were wrapped up in the same way that Hume had wrapped up his first victim. Evans had known about this from the newspaper reports that had been found in his room.

Christie used gas to incapacitate his victims, before raping them when unconscious and then strangling them. Beryl was not gassed and the marks on her body were not Christie's trademark. Beryl had been hit about the face; Christie did not do this but, as Lucy saw, Evans did. Timothy John Evans was the guilty man.

Jonathan agrees with me, although his dates differ, that the evidence against Evans is overwhelming. Timothy John Evans murdered Beryl and Geraldine.

Chapter 25
The Legacy of 10 Rillington Place

Around 1968, Lea and I decided to have a look at Rillington Place. I hadn't returned since the days Beryl lived there nearly 20 years earlier, and I wasn't sure how the visit would affect me. How would I cope with going to the site where my sister and niece were so brutally murdered? Since my frequent visits in the 1940s, I had only seen the street in photographs.

It was a warm, sunny day. We walked halfway down the street, and my eyes became fixed on the end house. The appalling memories were too much to bear.

Lea said she was overcome by a feeling of coldness and disbelief. We were looking at the very centre of the grief and sadness that had affected such a large part of my life from a young age.

The street seemed shorter and the houses looked so much smaller than I remembered. The name of the road had been changed to Ruston Close in May 1954, presumably to try to remove the stigma of its notoriety. It was still generally known by the previous name, though.

The area had been really brought down by Christie and Evans, and later the houses were all demolished and redeveloped. Many people went round to see if they could pick up any souvenirs from the rubble.

We returned again in the mid-80s to see what had been built following the redevelopment of Rillington Place.

There was quite a surprise in store. A number of 'town house' properties graced the left-hand side, while small workshop-type buildings had been constructed beneath the railway bridge. And Rillington Place, then Ruston Close, had acquired another new name. The street became known as Bartle Road in 1978.

As we walked down Bartle Road, we saw a memorial garden neatly lawned, paved and planted with trees and shrubs. What a difference it made. Our spirits lifted at once, and we were overcome with a sense of tranquillity.

The footprint of 10 Rillington Place lies diagonally beneath the modern buildings in St Andrew's Square, and the garden lies in front of where the old house once stood.

The developers thought no one would wish to find themselves living on the exact same spot where the former 10 Rillington Place had once been; they decided to change the whole design of the new development encompassing Bartle Road, St Andrew's

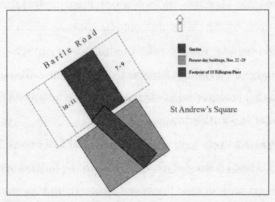

The memorial garden, showing its position in Bartle Road.

Square and Wesley Square. The plan was to erase all memories of the old Rillington Place and Ruston Close.

The late crime writer Ruth Rendell was intrigued by the Christie case, and visited Rillington Place after the rebuilding work. 'I knew that here was something which was a total contrast. You couldn't get further away from what had been here before.

'The case of John Reginald Halliday Christie has always interested me. He was an obnoxious man, a dreadful man. Perhaps one of the things that interested me so much was that people thought he was a good, virtuous, honest, upright citizen. He was also a marvellous hoaxer. By the way he talked and his authoritative manner, he made people believe he was halfway to a doctor, if not further.'

It wasn't so very long ago when Lea and I discovered Beryl and Geraldine's resting place. I had missed the funeral because I couldn't get back in time from New Zealand, and no one in the family recalled attending or even knowing the date.

We suddenly found out by accident where they were buried during our research of the case and the exhumation that had taken place in 1953.

There it was: Gunnersbury Cemetery. Soon afterwards we took a trip up to London to find their grave. We established that they had been buried together in the same coffin, mother and baby.

On arriving at the cemetery, we went into the office to ask where we might find the grave of Beryl and Geraldine Evans.

After explaining who we were, the relevant details were written down and handed to us.

It was quite a distance, way over the other side of the cemetery. To our amazement, the grave was in the Roman Catholic section, despite their Jewish heritage. That section of the cemetery was full of 'common graves': each of the hundreds of graves contained multiple interments. Six coffins per grave, in most cases.

A common grave has always been classed as a 'pauper's grave'. Today it would be referred to as a contract funeral or a welfare funeral, but by any name it amounts to the same thing: the deceased was buried by the state, because they either had no family or no money.

I was shocked to find that Dad had failed to ensure that Beryl and Geraldine had a dignified funeral. He had walked away, leaving it to someone else to arrange, so naturally nobody attended.

We believe that Beryl and Geraldine were buried on 12 December 1949. Our attempts so far to have their remains reburied privately have failed, mainly due to bureaucracy, but we will persevere.

At the time of writing, I am one of only a few people alive with first-hand knowledge about 10 Rillington Place. The judge, prosecutors, defence team and police officers are all long gone. The Proberts and Lynches are no longer with us.

Albert Pierrepoint, who hanged Evans and Christie, continued his trade until 1956 when he resigned after a dispute over fees when a convicted child killer was reprieved at the last minute. His memoirs were published in his book *Executioner: Pierrepoint*. On 10 July 1992, Albert died in a Southport nursing home at the age of 87.

As for his assistant, Syd Dernley, he was removed from the official list of executioners in 1954. Dernley said it was because he had commented on the size of a hanged man's private parts, but the more likely reason is that, the same year, he was jailed for six months after admitting publishing obscene books and photographs. The case involved a hangman's rope, an antique whip and people of high standing who could not possibly have their identities revealed. He later brought out a book, *The Hangman's Tale*, revealing the horrors of what happened when things went wrong during executions.

On 27 December 1957, our father William Thorley passed away in hospital aged 69.

Dad died with a troubled mind. He never got over the loss of Beryl and Geraldine in such traumatic circumstances. He also lived with the guilt that, had he acted sooner and brought them both down to Brighton, life would have been so different.

He was still married to Marguerita at the time of his death; she was never one to involve his family with anything. In her mind, we didn't exist.

A short while afterwards, Basil and I found a small life insurance policy that Dad had taken out years and years before.

It was one of those where the person paid a couple of pennies weekly, usually collected at the door, for about 100 years. The next of kin would probably be paid out the grand sum of £12 or so at the end.

We needed a copy of his death certificate to cash in the policy. We also needed a copy of his birth certificate. We went to acquire them from the records office at Somerset House in London, and we were in for a surprise or two.

Basil and I jumped on his BSA Bantam motorbike, which sounded a bit like an oversized hairdryer and had just about as much power. We got as far as Patcham, about three miles outside Brighton, when we stopped because of the freezing cold. It was early January, after all. We found a newsagent's shop, bought a selection of daily papers, and stuffed them down our jackets for some added warmth. We then carried on to London, a bit more insulated.

We explained to one of the clerks at Somerset House that we required copies of Dad's birth and death certificates. He was most helpful and we followed him to the balcony area where the records were kept. We couldn't believe how much was stored there; the scene was overwhelming.

He located and pulled out the file containing all Dad's information. We found it all fascinating, until we saw the marriage certificate. It read: William Clayton Thorley married Lizzie Bates on 13 April 1913. We knew that Dad had been married before our time, and we asked to see the marriage certificate of Dad to our mother, Elizabeth Simmonds. There wasn't one.

They were never married, and none of us had ever known. We asked for a copy of Mum's death certificate, and it was in the name of Thorley, not Simmonds. We wondered where this was leading.

We looked at each other with trepidation. Where did the dreaded Marguerita fit into all of this? Even the clerk was showing interest in what was now turning up. There was no dissolution of his marriage to Lizzie Thorley (née Bates) and no record of a marriage to Elizabeth Simmonds.

Then the final shock came. On reading the details of William Clayton Thorley's relationship with Marguerita Annie Burnard, we discovered that they had been married since 7 February 1948 at Brighton Register Office, only 11 months after our mother's death, and despite Dad's undissolved marriage to Lizzie Bates. Dad had produced the death certificate of our mother, in the name of Thorley not Simmonds, to marry Marguerita.

His condition was listed as 'bachelor'. In fact, Dad was an undiscovered bigamist.

Basil and I made it our mission before returning home to try to find where the original Mrs Lizzie Thorley, formerly Bates, lived. We couldn't believe our luck to find that she lived near Westbourne Park Road, an area we knew well, very close to Cambridge Gardens where we had all lived as a family so many years ago.

It was a strange feeling when we knocked at her front door and introduced ourselves as Thorleys. She asked if we were related to William and we said we were, explaining as briefly as possible the whole story. We suggested that it was more appropriate for her to have Dad's death certificate, as she would be rightfully entitled to the widow's pension.

The final wound for us as a family came from Dad's deceit, and the knowledge that all this had taken place before the family tragedy in November 1949.

My brother Basil died in Brighton, where he had lived for many years, on 31 October 2014, at the age of 83. Deep down, Basil knew that Evans was guilty of both murders. He seemed to change his mind from time to time, but ultimately he knew the truth.

My sister Pat was also badly affected by the murders of Beryl and Geraldine. The legacy of 10 Rillington Place cast a long, dark shadow over our lives and that would never go away.

Like the rest of us, Pat never really saw eye to eye with Marguerita. Within a few years of our move to Brighton, Pat met a young local lad, and they used to go about together until she found herself pregnant. She was only 16 years old, and I don't believe he was much older.

His mother made it quite clear that he had to cut off the relationship, and that was the end of a beautiful friendship. Pat had no mother of her own to advise or support her, and Dad wouldn't really have known what to do next anyway.

And so Pat gave birth to a healthy baby girl called Linda. Straight away, my thoughts flashed back to my days spent with Beryl and Geraldine. It must have been a frightening time for Pat, but she was a really good mum and coped extremely well under such trying circumstances.

As time went on she met Bill Yarlett, who was in the army doing his national service. They met up when they could and, when he was finally demobbed, they were able to get to know each other better. He was great with the baby and eventually they became man and wife.

Bill and Pat moved to a flat in Hove and set up home, by which time Bill had secured a job with British Rail, where he continued all his working life. He was based in London and eventually they decided to move up to Wandsworth.

Pat and Bill extended their family by having two more gorgeous daughters, Jackie and Debbie, and concluding their collection with a son, Richard.

Pat rarely spoke about Beryl and Geraldine at great length. She would tell people about when we were kids and what we used to get up to. She said her sister had died, but never went into the tragic details. It was as if she had shut down that episode in her life. We felt, perhaps, that was her way of dealing with the grief.

Meanwhile Pat became a Jehovah's Witness, which seemed to give her some comfort and peace, although it did take up a vast amount of her time. We could see that it was disrupting her marriage, because she was out so often, knocking on doors with the religious people. Bill resigned himself to the fact that he wasn't going to change her, as she became more and more involved. He used to tell us it was all right as long as it didn't prevent him going to his football matches.

Like many marriages, this one went through difficult times, and sadly it ended in divorce. Pat decided to move down to Brighton, where she could be near to Debbie and her grandchildren. Pat was happy in this new environment, and enjoyed holidays with them, even going abroad, something she had never done before.

In later life, Pat was diagnosed with early stages of Alzheimer's. It had a gradual, devastating effect. It was so sad to see, as there was nothing anyone could do – we all saw the frustration in her and felt helpless. Eventually all her powers of understanding and recognition disappeared. Pat passed on to a better place in August 2019, and is finally at peace.

Pat was proud of her family and they have been a credit to her. They showed their endless love in return, by the way they cared for her until the end.

* * *

The events at 10 Rillington Place continue to fascinate the public even today, and the questions around Evans's guilt or innocence have never gone away.

What about baby Geraldine? Has she been forgotten? How do people think the Thorley family dealt with their pain and shock after the loss of Beryl, Geraldine and her unborn son?

Evans's family still want the conviction quashed. There should be as much chance of that happening as we have of getting Beryl and Geraldine back.

I still have Beryl's wedding ring, that lasting memory of my treasured sister. I've kept it for 70 years in a special place, tucked into a drawer with my other precious possessions – a very special place for a very special ring.

A poignant reminder of a big sister I loved so much. And I will take that ring to my grave.

References

Oates, Jonathan. John Christie of Rillington Place: Pen & Sword Books Ltd., 2012.

Curnow, John. The Murders, Myths and Reality of 10 Rillington Place: Progress Publishing, 2016.

Pierrepoint, Albert. Executioner: Pierrepoint: Coronet Books, 1977.

Kennedy, Ludovic. Ten Rillington Place: Gollancz, 1961.

Eddowes, John. The Two Killers of Rillington Place: Warner Books, 1995.

Peter lays flowers at the grave of Beryl and Geraldine on what would have been his sister's 90th birthday.

Acknowledgements

To my family and very close friends, your love and support has been the driving force in the compilation of this book.

Thank you to my wife Lea who carried out the research over 35 years and for her tireless work in helping to prepare this book.

I would also like to thank the following people who were an immense help: author David Meikle, Iain Tidey, Jonathan Oates, John Curnow, Kate Beal, Richard Plews and our children.

If this book can show people that the truth is out there, and it has been discovered, then that gives me some comfort. Of course, nothing can change the fact that our family is still in mourning.

We will be grieving for ever.